Jennie + Esteban,

God has
BIG plans
for you.

Dann Wilkins

Ashley Wilkins

PRAISE FOR
THE COUNTERFEIT CLIMAX

"Dave and Ashley have worked together to create such an amazing resource for couples. Sexual issues are one of the most controversial subjects discussed in marriage. This resource addresses each and every question most couples are too hesitant to ask. Their answers are so clinically sound, practically possible, and immediately applicable. I highly recommend this book whether you are single, engaged, married, divorced, or anywhere in between."

—**Dr. Cassie Reed**, LPC-Supervisor, Director Marriage and Family Therapy, Associate Professor of Counseling, The King's University

"Honest. So, so honest! These are sensitive but important conversations the church (and others) need to be having. The authenticity with which Dave and Ashley write, as they communicate through the lenses of Scripture and their own personal struggles, takes what should be complex and uncomfortable topics and makes them simple and disarming, providing hope for every reader."

—**Dr. Beau Hummel,** President/Co-Founder, Marriage For Life, Inc.

"Dave and Ashley Willis are some of the most authentic and genuine people I know. And that shows in this book. I love how they're open about some really hard topics and give great Biblical insight into how to have a marriage that honors God."

—**Joël Malm,** Founder, Summit Leaders, Author, *Love Slows Down*

"Dave and Ashley Willis are such a fun and real couple. I highly recommend reading anything they've written, as it's written with love, experience, and a realistic approach. This book is a must have for any couple that wants to connect on a real level. "

—**Brandi Rhodes,** Model, Wrestler, and Reality TV Star

"There is no doubt that God has raised Dave and Ashley up to be the leading voices for healthy, vulnerable, strong marriages. *The Counterfeit Climax* is such a valuable resource filled with raw and unfiltered truth that has been wrapped in genuine love and grace. We encourage you to read these words with an open heart, mind, and spirit so they will bring healing, joy, and strength to your most prized relationship."

—**Clayton & Ashlee Hurst,** Marriage Pastors, Lakewood Church

"We live in a culture built on counterfeit claims about sex and marriage, which has led many to experience a life of dissatisfaction and even despair. This book is not only a course correction for so many who are wandering in cultural fallacies but a beautiful invitation into a story of God's loving design for sex and marriage. I fully believe that as you read this book, you will be drawn deeper into a life of true joy, satisfaction, and intimacy."

—**Nirup Alphonse,** Lead Pastor, Lifegate Church Denver

"*The Counterfeit Climax* is a book that powerfully addresses the deep issues and false misconceptions of sex that couples in marriage are facing today. In a world that is engulfed with a spiritual darkness attacking the mind and heart about sex, Dave and Ashley guide you into God's truth about His perfect design for marital intimacy. They give practical insight into taking the gospel into your sex life. We truly believe that this book will serve to strengthen and cultivate a healthy marriage and mindset about sex. We love this book and highly recommend it to anyone seeking to transform their marital intimacy."

—**Scott & Vanessa Martindale,** Founders,
Blended Kingdom Families Ministries

"Dave and Ashley have written a transparent dose of truth for anyone wanting sexual intimacy. It's a must-read for your relationship."

—**Sean & Lanette Reed,** Authors, *Marriage in Transition*,
Marriage Pastors, Opendoor Church

THE

COUNTERFEIT

CLIMAX

FOREWORD BY
JONATHAN "JP" POKLUDA

Bestselling Author of *Outdated: Find Love That Lasts When Dating Has Changed*

THE

COUNTERFEIT

CLIMAX

CONFRONTING THE ISSUES THAT SABOTAGE
SEX, ROMANCE, AND RELATIONSHIPS

BESTSELLING AUTHORS
DAVE & ASHLEY WILLIS

CONTENTS

FOREWORD

My wife and I got married in a chapel in Texas. I remember when the door flung open in the back, and I saw her in her dress for the first time. I could hardly catch my breath as the beautiful scene quickly blurred with my tears. As she joined me at the altar, we made some rather crazy promises to each other: "…for richer or poorer, in sickness and in health, until death do us part." After our kiss, we walked down the aisle, fists pumping the air, with big goofy grins on our faces. In the foyer of the chapel, as soon as we were alone, I held her in my arms and prayed this prayer: "Dear God, thank You for this day. Thank You for my wife, and thank You for allowing me to escape the consequences of my sins." When I said, "consequences of my sins," I was thinking specifically of my sexual sins. I was referring to the many sexual partners I'd had, the boundaries my wife and I had crossed, my personal purity, and my addiction to pornography. That feels like a long list. But it seemed to me, in that moment, that I got away with it. I had not.

Two years into marriage, I realized the naivety of my prayer. I hadn't escaped the consequences; they just came in a very different form than anticipated. I had no idea how to love one person. I had no idea how to be selfless. The desire for porn was still there—turns out marriage doesn't take that away. My wife struggled with shame from our dating life and didn't feel the freedom in marriage I'd hoped she would. I thought marriage would be one long bedroom session every night—and again in the morning on most days. It was not. I was dealing with anger from some missed expectations.

I vacillated back and forth from thinking I was ruined by my previous choices to believing they shouldn't impact marriage at all. I'd heard that "if you go over the fence to steal the fruit, it doesn't taste as sweet when you enter through the gate." It felt like our marriage was cursed by our past.

The truth is, everything we do before marriage impacts our marriage. Things like our family of origin, our parents' marriage, our dating life, our sex life, our personal purity, our theology, and even movies we've seen, images we've looked at, and stories we've read. *Everything*. While our sin always has consequences, we are never beyond hope. We just needed a guide to help us find the intimacy God intended for us to have in marriage. And when we find one, our marriages can move to a place of incredible health and joy.

If you've found yourself wondering if there could be a better marriage out there, you're in the right place. You need a guide to help you find the intimacy you hoped for but might be apprehensive about. That guide will need to be absolutely honest, really candid, fully transparent, very experienced, and unquestionably knowledgeable when it comes to God's desires for sex and marriage. I believe Dave and Ashley Willis can be just those guides for you. They have lived it, seen it, counseled it, and helped so many find joy in their relationships.

The pages ahead are not filled with restrictions that seek to steal your joy. In fact, the pages ahead are filled with permissions to give you and your spouse liberty to enjoy each other to the glory of God. My friends, hold nothing back when addressing any issues that come up as you read, and I believe you will really appreciate their honest approach. So many people are going to be helped by this resource. When you are one of them, please share it with other married friends you care about. The struggles Dave and Ashley address are ones that steal joy from most married couples. Do NOT settle for a counterfeit climax. Search out the real thing in the pages ahead.

Jonathan "JP" Pokluda
Best-selling Author & Lead Pastor
of Harris Creek Baptist Church

INTRODUCTION

DEFINING THE
COUNTERFEIT CLIMAX

Ernest Hemingway was one of the most gifted writers and fascinating personalities of the 20th Century. He lived a life of unbelievable adventure, and he experienced nearly every form of success the world has to offer, but he never found long-term success in his relationships. His well-funded adventures were a diversion from his ongoing relationship drama, but he never seemed to find real happiness. Instead, he adopted a pessimistic view of happiness and once famously said, "Happiness among intelligent people is the rarest thing on earth."

On a cruise ship stop in Key West, Florida, many years ago, we had the opportunity to visit and tour his home, which is perpetually preserved as a museum to his life and legacy. As part of the tour, the guide pointed out what he referred to as "The Wall of Wives." It was a section of portraits and photographs showing the many women who had been romantically involved with Hemingway over the years. Our guide joked about the number of women on the wall, but his jokes seemed to display his own respect for Hemingway's sexual prowess more than an acknowledgment of his dysfunctional lifestyle.

The guide pointed to the ladies' pictures and, one by one, told us the short version of each relationship. Some of these women had been wives. Some had been girlfriends. Some had been mistresses. Some had been a quick dalliance, while others had been fairly long relationships. One thing they all had in common? They all ended. He had lived for pleasure, only to find that pleasure without love becomes a prison. Tragically, Hemingway took his own life and died a single man.

As we learned more of his life story and started to piece together the broken track record of these relationships, we saw some of the same broken mindsets in Hemingway that we see throughout our modern culture. Like millions of others, Hemingway believed in a counterfeit version of love, and his sex life was a continuous pursuit of counterfeit climaxes. First off, he seemed addicted to the rush of the early stages of a relationship, but he had little interest in the ongoing work every relationship requires. Once the newness wore off, he found himself feeling bored or trapped.

Once he found himself feeling bored or trapped, he would escape. Sometimes those escapes would be through a breakup, but often the relationship would continue limping along, and he'd frequently escape through an affair, his work, or a hobby. He became an avid deep-sea fisherman, a hobby that took him away from home for long stretches of time. We wonder if it was his love for fish or his desire to avoid the drama at home that kept him on his boat so often.

He also found more solace in relationships with his pets (cats) and drinking buddies than in his romantic partnerships. This is still a common form of avoidance for many married people today. We often encounter couples who treat their pets better than their spouses and who spend more time building friendships with the guys at the golf club or the ladies at book club than they spend investing in their friendship with their spouse.

We share this story right at the beginning of the book because we see many of Hemingway's broken patterns playing out in marriages today. Although he lived generations ago, his struggles are just as relevant in our own generation. Like so many of us today, Hemingway settled for what we call a "counterfeit climax." When we refer to the counterfeit climax, we are referring to every sexual mindset, sexual relationship, and sexual experience fueled by false beliefs or impure motives that sabotage real intimacy and replace it with a cheapened, artificial version of sex.

> **When we refer to the counterfeit climax, we are referring to every sexual mindset, sexual relationship, and sexual experience fueled by false beliefs or impure motives that sabotage real intimacy and replace it with a cheapened, artificial version of sex.**

The counterfeit climax has infiltrated its way into nearly every life and every marriage, and in its wake, we experience confusion, baggage, shame, and frustration. It gives temporary pleasure in exchange for permanent regret and even disillusionment.

Some counterfeit climaxes pursued by Hemingway and millions of others include:

* Pursuing sexual pleasure without sexual monogamy and commitment.
* Valuing a variety of partners over cultivating deep intimacy with one partner.

* Allowing past regrets to sabotage present relationships.
* Defining love in superficial or selfish terms.
* Basing our relational health on our feelings instead of our principles.
* Selfishly putting our own desires ahead of our spouse's needs.
* Desiring a high quantity of orgasms over a high quality of connection.
* Walking away from marriage the moment it becomes difficult.
* Using a partner's body without adoring their soul.
* Fueling our sexual appetites with fantasies that have no basis in reality.
* Allowing our own insecurities to sabotage sexual intimacy in marriage.
* Believing the wrong voices, which distorts our thinking about sex.

Countless couples who write to us for help have fallen into these same traps and believed the same counterfeit stories about love and sex. Instead of doing the ongoing work to keep the marriage thriving, one or both spouses have believed the myth: *"If I married the 'right' person, the relationship shouldn't take work. It should all happen naturally. All of my needs and fantasies would be met if only my spouse would do their part or leave so I could go find someone who will finally fulfill these desires."*

When we allow Hollywood, pop culture, romance novels, porn, or anything at all other than the Bible, to shape our view of sex, we're going to end up with distorted perspectives. So much of the modern narrative about love and marriage makes people believe it's all about feelings, and, once your feelings change, then you should abandon the relationship and go look for those feelings on your own with someone new. Our modern culture encourages us that we need to find "our truth" (whatever that means) to be happy.

We are wrongly taught that our own pursuit of happiness is more sacred than our covenant of marriage, and millions of families have been ripped apart because a spouse decided that they would be happier in another arrangement. We're not saying that there's never a time for divorce, nor are we trying to shame anyone who has experienced divorce. We're simply saying that as a culture, we've developed some broken values when it comes to sex and marriage, and those broken values have created far too many divorces. When it comes to love, countless people are following Hemingway's plan instead of Jesus' plan. Our world has largely abandoned God's perfect plan for sex and replaced it with counterfeit forms of love and sex.

The number of couples dealing with some form of sexual frustration is staggering. In fact, we would argue that every couple faces sex-related struggles from time to time. For some couples, the perpetual tension caused by these issues is the single greatest obstacle in their marriage.

> **Our world has largely abandoned God's perfect plan for sex and replaced it with counterfeit forms of love and sex.**

Multiple times a day, listeners of *The Naked Marriage* podcast and those who follow us on social media send us emails and private messages like these:

> My husband wants to have sex all the time, but I don't have any drive at all. I love my husband, but I'm just not really interested in sex. We still do it occasionally, but my husband lives in constant sexual frustration and then gets angry with me. I'm not sure what to do. He says we're more like roommates than husband and wife, and he wants a wife, not a roommate. I want a good marriage too. What do we do?—Amy B.

> I've watched porn since I was a kid. It has shaped my views about sex. I've finally broken away from my porn addiction, but I can't seem to break away from wanting my wife to do certain acts and fetishes that I learned through porn. I have a hard time even getting aroused if she won't do those certain things, but it makes her feel dirty when she does it. Our sex life (and our marriage) is really struggling, and we don't know how to move past it.—Jake P.

> Before we were married, I had multiple sexual partners, but my husband was a virgin. We talked through everything as we prepared for marriage, and he seemed totally fine with my past, but now, it's clear that he's not

fine with it. He's very insecure about my past sexual partners, and he's always asking me questions about them or about what specific things we did in bed. He accuses me of comparing him to these past lovers and makes cutting remarks. I love my husband, and I can't change the past, but I can't seem to do anything to make my husband know my heart is his. I'm totally committed to my husband, but sometimes he talks to me like I'm trash and I can't take it anymore.—Jenn R.

I was sexually abused as a kid, but I've never been able to tell my wife about it. The memories still haunt me. Sometimes, I even get flashbacks when my wife and I are making love, and she knows something is wrong, but I always make other excuses. I don't want her to look at me differently, and I'm afraid to tell her. Should I tell her? How do I tell her?—Chris W.

I've gained weight since we were first married, and I'm really self-conscious of my body. I don't like to be naked or even for my husband to watch me get dressed or undressed. He always says how much he loves my body, and he practically begs to see me, but when we do make love, I can't be comfortable unless the room is totally dark. I go out of my way to not let my husband see me. I can tell it really hurts his feelings, but I just can't get past my insecurities. My husband feels rejected, but he doesn't seem to understand how I'm feeling. I wish I could just be free with my body in the bedroom, but I don't know how.—Molly L.

My wife and I were both accustomed to taking care of our own sexual needs before we got together. I masturbated daily, and she always had the most technologically advanced vibrator on her bedside table. When we got married, we realized that we'd each gotten so good at meeting our own needs that we were really bad at meeting each other's needs in bed. Sex became a selfish act for both of us, and it has caused a lot of frustration. We're trying to both break the habit of masturbation and do a better job of being selfless lovers by putting each other's needs first, but it's like we're learning to walk for the first time. We keep tripping over ourselves. How do we break out of the negative cycle and actually have a great sex life?—Carlos A.

I grew up in a family and in a church where sex was always talked about in a negative way. I kind of shut off the sexual part of myself completely. Once I got married, I didn't know how to turn on the sexual side of me. I still feel dirty every time we do it. My husband can tell I don't enjoy it, and this is heartbreaking for him. I know it sounds crazy, but every time we're making love, I just picture my parents, my youth pastor, and even God all watching me, shaking their heads in disgust. I don't know how to get past my hang-ups.—Melissa B.

All of these messages come from different perspectives and address different issues, but they're all united by some common themes. All of these people are facing struggles in their marriages that stem from frustrations, misconceptions, and/ or baggage related to sex. So many couples wrestle with issues and mindsets that negatively impact their sex lives and their marriages. They also suffer from isolation because they don't know where they can safely find answers to these important questions. We hope this book is a safe place where you can find answers to many of these questions. When you cultivate a healthy new mindset about sex, we believe every aspect of your marriage (both inside and outside the bedroom) will improve.

It's time to fight back and replace that sexual baggage with sexual fulfillment. God has given us a beautiful and timeless roadmap for real intimacy and sex. As you learn to apply His perfect principles meant to guide the powerful gift of sex, you'll experience healing, freedom, pleasure, and intimate connection within marriage. Once you've learned to experience sex the way God intended, you'll never want to settle for a counterfeit climax again.

This book will address countless counterfeits that have become widely believed. Especially within the church, we've found that many Christians don't feel equipped to have healthy conversations to confront these counterfeit mindsets. We hope this book leads to breakthrough within cultures, churches, and homes and brings about conversations that are long overdue. More than anything, we hope it sparks a new era of healing and health in your own life and marriage.

It's time to recommit to God's timeless plan for relationships instead of the counterfeits force-fed to us by our modern culture. It's time to dispel the myths we've believed about love and then work to undo the damage those destructive mindsets have caused in our marriages and families. It's time to unlearn the lies and relearn the truth. It's time to readjust our compasses, so we can know for certain that we're heading in the right direction.

It's important to note that there is both bad news *and* good news in all of this. The bad news is the counterfeit messages are probably even more pervasive than you may realize, and we've all been impacted by them. The good news is the solutions probably aren't as complicated as you imagine. Most people in our modern world tend to view love, sex, and marriage through the lens of that one phrase that became popular when Facebook added their relationship status feature years ago: "It's complicated." The truth is that while healthy relationships take a lot of work, the formula for making them work is actually much simpler than you might have imagined. God gives us a timeless roadmap for sex and for healthy marriages in the Bible, and once we learn it and apply it, while there's still daily work to be done to invest in the relationship, it's not nearly as complicated or drama-filled as our culture has taught us.

While marriage itself may not be overly complicated, the world's approach to relationships remains incredibly complicated (and broken). The confusing messages fed to us about sex, gender, marriage, porn, romance, and love can make our heads spin. We want to help you cut through the noise and clutter of all the counterfeit messages in our complicated world and rediscover the beautiful truths of God's perfect design for sex and marriage. In doing so, we believe you'll find a formula for a healthy marriage and a healthy mindset, so you can experience the fullness of God's design for marital intimacy. Getting there might require unlearning some false messages you've been taught to believe. It might also require relearning (or learning for the first time) God's timeless principles in these areas. It won't necessarily be easy, but it will be worth it.

We are honored to be on this journey with you. In all of life, there's no more sacred quest than the quest for healthy relationships. The timeless truths from Scriptures, stats, and stories on the pages to come can help you in that sacred journey. There's a great adventure ahead, and we believe that it will lead you toward more healing and wholeness. We are praying for you and cheering you on every step of the way!

—Dave and Ashley
daveandashleywillis.com

CHAPTER 1

THE INVENTOR OF SEX

When you look around our current culture, everywhere you turn, there are examples of people misusing God's gift of sex. In fact, sex may be the one thing in our world that has been most often counterfeited with false, damaging lies. The notion that sex is created for a lifelong, monogamous commitment between one husband and one wife is treated with contempt as an archaic and out-of-touch approach. Under the guise of enlightenment and progress, we've defined sex on our own terms and then ignored the obvious consequences our sexual rebellion has created. Every human on earth has been negatively impacted in some way by the misuse of sex.

We want to share an example from history about a group of people with good ideas and good motives who completely missed the point when it came to sex. In missing the point about sex, their movement died altogether. Instead of erring on the modern extreme of promiscuity, they made the mistake of championing chastity to the point of convincing many that *all* sex is inherently wrong.

Growing up in Central Kentucky, we were surrounded by natural beauty and horse farms, but there weren't a lot of exciting tourist destinations, so a picturesque place in Harrodsburg, Kentucky called "Shakertown" stood out as something novel. Dave and I

Sex may be the one thing in our world that has been most often counterfeited with false, damaging lies.

didn't know each other as kids, but at some point in our elementary school years, both of our public schools made a field trip to visit Shakertown and learn the history of this unique and mysterious group known as the Shakers.

The Shakers were pioneers in gender equality and creating an egalitarian community where men and women shared the responsibilities of leadership with no stigmas or limitations defining what a girl could grow up to become. Centuries ago, their ideas were radical and revolutionary. There's much to applaud about the Shakers. Their work ethic and craftsmanship were unparalleled. They saw their work as a form of worship and did everything to the glory of God. This commitment to excellence is probably why their buildings and even much of their furniture endures centuries after being built.

We can also commend their desire to live out their Christian faith as a community of equality. They chose to see the inherent value in every person and recognized all people—men and women—as being of equal worth and coheirs as sons and daughters in God's kingdom. In that way, their lifestyle was a tiny glimpse of heaven. They also worshipped unabashedly by raising their hands and shaking their whole bodies as they sang to the Lord, which led them to be called the Shakers.

For all the many positive attributes we can see in the Shakers, there were also some very troubling aspects of their belief system. While they championed the value and equality of men and women at a time when so few shared those sentiments, worked hard, and lived out their faith, they didn't value marriage. They adopted an unhealthy view of marriage that effectively sabotaged their otherwise healthy views.

When a married couple decided to join the Shakers, they had to enter the community as a brother and sister in Christ and as a brother and sister with the others in the village. They were no longer allowed to function as a married couple. The Shakers required strict separation of men and women. While both men and women shared in leadership and were treated with equality, they were also treated separately.

Men and women lived in separate buildings. They ate at separate tables. They worshiped on separate sides of the sanctuary. They even had separate doors for entering and exiting. They also didn't believe in sex. We've often joked that's why they were always shaking: sexual frustration!

The Shakers sought equality through separation. In this way, they missed the mark because true equality can only exist within the context of people working together in healthy relationships. We can never find true equality apart from relationships because relationships are the purpose of life.

You can admire someone without knowing them or interacting with them. We admire plenty of famous people we'll never meet, but respect and love are different. Respect and love can't exist apart from relationships. These are not abstract concepts but real-life expressions of our souls that can only be given and received from real-life people in real-life ways. This type of love and respect doesn't just happen through healthy beliefs; it always requires healthy relationships.

It's probably no surprise to you that the Shaker movement died out, and all that remains are the remnants of their buildings, handmade furniture, and school children on field trips learning about their strange way of life. It turns out that forcing celibacy isn't a great recruitment tool, and it also does nothing to create future generations through childbearing. Still, it's a beautiful place to visit if you ever find yourself in Central Kentucky.

We want to be a part of a movement that shares the Shakers' vision for gender equality but finds ways to live out that vision in relationships instead of in segregation. As we raise our four sons, we want them to see that true respect for women must exist in healthy relationships *with* women. In school, in the workplace, in friendships, and, eventually, in marriage, respect for women doesn't happen from a distance; it happens in relationships.

> When we avoid talking about sex, nobody wins. In the vacuum our silence creates, people are either tempted to demonize sex or miss out on the God-given beauty of it in marriage or go to the other extreme and live a life of promiscuity.

When we avoid talking about sex, nobody wins. In the vacuum our silence creates, people are either tempted to demonize sex or miss out on the God-given beauty of it in marriage or go to the other extreme and live a life of promiscuity. Sex is a powerful gift, and when misused, it can create great pain and disrespect.

But when enjoyed in the right context, it's one of the greatest gifts God has given us. Much of the baggage so many adults have related to sex comes from this same distorted message that sex itself is somehow bad or "dirty." We need to redeem that lie with the truth that sex is a beautiful, God-created gift designed to be enjoyed within the lifelong covenant of marriage.

Sex on Campus

We've seen that many of the counterfeit messages about sex in our culture are being taught on college and university campuses. These false lessons are sometimes taught in the classroom, but more often, they're taught through a broken cultural system of sexual exploration among the students. Just down the road from Shakertown in a Communication Studies graduate course on the University of Kentucky campus, I (Dave) remember sitting around a circle with other graduate students, listening with shock to the new research findings of our professor. Dr. Alan D. Desantis was one of the most talented, entertaining, and eclectic educators I ever had. He was also an advisor for some of the fraternities and sororities on campus, and he was leveraging his knowledge of Greek life—as a former frat guy himself and now as an advisor—to do an in-depth analysis of gender roles and sexual behaviors of modern college students in fraternities and sororities. His research opened my eyes to the widespread culture of sex-based disrespect happening on university campuses.

He started the discussion by explaining that there had been a long history in fraternities of organizing events, often under the guise of social mixers or fundraisers, with the primary objective of convincing young women to perform for them. In other words, the frat boys felt entitled to disrespect these young women, all in the name of fun and entertainment. This performance-based expectation of females often crossed lines into expectations of sexual performance. He later summed up all these findings in a groundbreaking research study and book entitled, *Inside Greek U.: Fraternities, Sororities, and the Pursuit of Power, Pleasure, and Prestige.*[1]

Of all the findings his multiyear research yielded, none was more troubling than the sexual climate on campuses and, specifically, the sexual objectification of women. College men seemed pleased to play the role of a feminist, and then, under the guise of female empowerment, these men would pour strong drinks, create festive atmospheres, and do whatever they could to bed as many young women as possible.

Even when intercourse wasn't taking place, young men became crafty in the art of coercion by convincing young women to perform other sexual acts, such as oral sex and anal sex. These men would use a woman's body for their own sexual gratification while at the same time praising the young woman for her chastity, class, and "technical virginity."

Dr. Desantis's research results were also in line with comments I heard while studying and teaching at multiple universities. Those experiences unearthed troubling statements like this:

---

1 Alan D. Desantis, *Inside Greek U: Fraternities, Sororities, and the Pursuit of Pleasure, Power, and Prestige* (Lexington: University Press of Kentucky, 2007), 69.

The classier a girl is in public, the more she wants to be treated like a whore in the bedroom. It's all a game. I treat classy girls like whores, and I treat whores like classy girls. It takes their guards down, and they end up doing whatever I want in the bedroom. —Chase E. (age 21)

Most girls don't actually mean 'no' when they say it. The hard-to-get routine is all part of the seduction. They act unwilling just because they know it's a turn-on for a guy if the girl seems like more of a challenge. They want to have it both ways: They want sex as much as guys do, but they also want to be seen as proper or whatever. Girls want sex even if they say they don't.—Jake K. (age 20)

Being an empowered woman means being sexually aggressive. A powerful woman realizes that her sexuality is part of her superpower over men. She might play the submissive role when it helps her get what she wants, but she's really the one in control. Porn becomes really instructive because it shows women how to find what they like and how to seduce men. The seducer is the one who is in control. An empowered woman is not afraid to use men to get what she wants because men have been using women since the beginning of time. It's time to flip the script. —Kristy P. (age 19)

Even with all the political and policy attention being directed at these issues on university campuses, the problems persist because it takes more than policy changes to make a difference and to heal from our own sexual baggage. It takes heart change.

I was on a college campus recently, and I saw a young woman wearing a shirt with the slogan, "Got Consent?" It has become a popular campaign on campuses to try to turn the tide of sexual assault and unwanted sexual aggression toward women. On the same day, a guy with a sick and inappropriate sense of humor wore another popular fraternity tee-shirt slogan, which seems to be an inappropriate, misogynistic, and misguided counterpoint to the "Got Consent?" campaign. His shirt said, "No means Yes. Yes, means anal!"

For all you parents of younger kids reading this, I promise I'm not trying to terrify you with these extreme examples of sexual brokenness on our university campuses. I'm not trying to convince you to homeschool your kids until they're thirty years old. I understand the instinct we have to protect our children, but we also need to prepare our children to live out their faith and values in a broken world. First, we must take a long, hard look at our personal beliefs about sex, so we can process and heal from our own sexual baggage.

> **We must take a long, hard look at our personal beliefs about sex, so we can process and heal from our own sexual baggage.**

Even if you have made compromises or fallen into a cycle of sexual sin, in the past or in the present, God's grace is always bigger than our biggest sin. Your poor choices don't have to define your future. Even if you made choices in college you now regret, those mistakes don't define you, and you shouldn't let them sabotage your peace, your identity, or your marriage.

The Right Message About Sex

Far too many parents, churches, and educators have taught an untrue and harmful message about sex. In an attempt to keep kids from delving into risky, early sexual exploration, sex itself is often demonized in our discussions. Maybe you grew up with Shakertown-baggage from being taught sex was dirty. Perhaps you can relate to the examples we just shared about dysfunctional and destructive attitudes about sex on campus. Maybe your own regrets are holding you back from enjoying sex right now.

Regardless of your own sexual baggage and the wrong lessons you may have been taught about sex, we all need to be reminded regularly that sex is a gift. It's beautiful. It was God's idea. Once people get a glimpse of God's perfect plan for sex, the quest for His best gifts will make the counterfeits of sexual sin seem unattractive in comparison.

A promiscuous lifestyle certainly should be avoided at all costs, but in our pious attempt to avoid promiscuity, we've thrown the proverbial baby out with the bathwater and have adopted a Shaker-like condemnation of all sex. We need to stop making "sex" a dirty word.

Without understanding the broader context that God's plan for sex is beautiful, many of us grew up seeing sex as something negative, and then when we started having sexual feelings, we believed there was something wrong with us. This set us up for sexual failure and shame. I am not trying to throw our parents under the bus here because I believe this teaching (or lack thereof) about the dangers of sex was done with good intentions. However, it was poorly executed and didn't yield healthy results. It's easier to slap a negative label on something than it is to have a dialogue that might lead to awkward questions and possibly even confessions about personal sexual history and past sins. That's scary, but it's worth the awkwardness to discover what it means to be naked and unashamed.

We didn't come up with this phrase, "naked and unashamed." It's actually God's idea. All great ideas are really His. We might try to reword things or get retweeted for saying something clever, but He's the creator of all good things, including sex.

When God first created man and woman in His own image, He made the man and his wife naked, and the Bible tells us in Genesis 2:25 that they were "naked and not ashamed." We love that imagery. We love that one of the first lessons the Bible teaches is that God has a beautiful plan for sex and marriage, and while deceivers might do much damage in creating counterfeit plans for sex, God's timeless design is still for complete love, intimacy, vulnerability, pleasure, acceptance, and joy. He still wants us to be naked and unashamed. God is the inventor of sex, and He wants sex

> **It's easier to slap a negative label on something than it is to have a dialogue that might lead to awkward questions and possibly even confessions about personal sexual history and past sins.**

to be one of the greatest gifts in our lives when enjoyed within a healthy marriage.

Along with the amazing team at XO Marriage, we talk about this concept often in our marriage ministry. At marriage conferences and churches all over America, we've talked to couples about our own story, hang-ups, and baggage, and God's redemptive love and grace in our marriage. You can read about our story and how to be naked and unashamed in our book, *The Naked Marriage*.

We believe that a naked marriage isn't just physical. The Bible's imagery of nakedness applies to all aspects of life. Nakedness is a picture of transparency and vulnerability. God wants us to enter marriage with no secrets and nothing to hide. He wants us with nothing up our sleeves because we're not wearing any sleeves! God wants you to enjoy the fullness of sexual pleasure and intimacy within your marriage. He wants you to find freedom from your own past hurts and hang-ups so you can enjoy the gift of sex the way He intended.

Embracing Freedom

One of our goals on *The Naked Marriage* podcast is to be a safe place to have honest conversations about sex. We've found that many people (especially our fellow Christians) have never felt like they had a safe space to ask honest questions about sex. When we can't talk honestly and openly about our needs, desires, regrets, fantasies, insecurities, curiosities, and everything else, shame takes the place of freedom, but God wants you to have freedom.

We recently received a message from a podcast listener who's been married for seventeen years. She said that while things are decent in their marriage overall, she and her husband had been in a rut for a long time. She felt like her needs weren't being met, and her husband was always complaining about his sexual frustration. Both spouses were frustrated when it came to sex, and they weren't sure if they'd ever break out of this rut. There hadn't been a "spark" in their marriage in a long time.

This listener credited one specific podcast episode with being the biggest difference-maker they'd ever experienced. She said it was a breakthrough and had sparked more fun, joy, intimacy, and excitement than anything they'd experienced in years. We were genuinely surprised when she said the episode that had created all this excitement was our episode on oral sex.

She explained that the episode had given them permission to talk very openly about what they each wanted in the bedroom. It challenged her to prioritize her husband's needs, so she started being intentional about prioritizing sex. In turn, her husband became much more romantic and attentive to her needs. Both of them were blown away by how they had gone from autopilot to red hot in their marriage, both inside and outside the bedroom. Maybe you need to put this book down for a minute and go listen to that oral sex episode on our podcast! It just might help you like it helped this couple.

We're passionate about helping married couples become naked and unashamed in the bedroom because that's God's design for marriage. He wants you to cut through all the counterfeit messages so you can experience blissful freedom, pleasure, and intimacy in the bedroom. As we wrap up this chapter, I (Dave) want to share one final story just to bring a smile to your face at my own expense and to celebrate the gift of nakedness when it's in the right context.

A few years ago, I found myself in the hospital for a minor surgery. I was nervously fidgeting in a holding room wearing a hospital gown that covered almost nothing and was about to cover even less, given the exposure and nudity that would soon be required. The painkiller they'd given me beforehand was already taking effect and, though my mind was still sharp, I could tell my body was starting to tingle with numbness. I would rather have been asleep altogether because I'm a pretty modest person, and I was about to assume a position that would make anyone blush.

> **He wants you to cut through all the counterfeit messages so you can experience blissful freedom, pleasure, and intimacy in the bedroom.**

There's something about being in a hospital gown that makes you feel pretty powerless and inspires you to call on a higher power, so I decided to say two prayers. The first prayer was that the procedure itself would go well and be painless. I wasn't too concerned about that part, so I spent more time on the second prayer.

The next prayer went something like this: "Lord, I'm about to be naked. You know that I wholeheartedly believe women can do things as well as men, oftentimes better than men. But today, I'd really appreciate it if no women were in this room.

Other than my wife, I'd just rather not have a woman seeing me like this. And one more thing: please don't let me know any of the people in that room, and, if I can get really specific, I'd prefer to never run into them again after the procedure. I would prefer not to see a guy at the grocery store and have to make small talk after they've seen me stark naked. Thanks, Lord. Amen."

I felt confident that God was going to take care of me on this prayer, but I was also feeling some regret that I hadn't driven to an out-of-town doctor's office for the procedure. They wheeled me into the room, and as I was contorted into an uncomfortable posture exposing more than I ever thought I'd be exposing in a well-lit public room, I looked around and saw there were only two men. I didn't recognize either of them. There wasn't a woman in sight.

Other than feeling like a bizarre, embarrassing dream, everything was going as well as could be expected. I took a deep breath and silently whispered a "thank you" prayer, but before I could finish it, an energetic female nurse burst into the room holding a clipboard and got a good look at my undercarriage before noticing my frightened face. When we made eye contact (which I was desperately trying to avoid), she nearly dropped her clipboard and exclaimed, "Pastor Dave! Oh my gosh! What are you doing here?"

I felt the answer to her question was obvious, so I opted not to answer. I'm not sure I would have had time to answer anyway because she immediately continued. "Dave, you probably don't know me, but I'm Donna. I go to your church, and I love hearing your sermons! Your book, *The Seven Laws of Love,* is one of my all-time favorite books."

She then turned her attention to the men in the room and began a very effective sales pitch, trying to get them to read my blogs and books. If she ever quits her nursing job, she'd make an amazing promoter. I thought about trying to hire her to do publicity for this book, but I made a pact with myself never to contact her or make eye contact with her again.

Donna said her goodbyes, and I managed to smile and wave from my awkward position. As the door closed behind her, I could hear her announce from the other side of the door, "Hey, girls, Pastor Dave is in there!"

I frantically looked around the room for a window or another exit I could use after the procedure, but, unfortunately, there was only one way out. When it was finished, I was wheeled out of the room to the waves and smiles from a throng of well-wishers, but it felt more like a gauntlet of paparazzi. I thought about changing my name and identity, but, after looking into the complicating logistics of it, opted instead to just wear hats and sunglasses in public for a while. Just kidding, but I don't plan to darken the door of that office again anytime soon.

Ashley and I had a good laugh in the waiting room afterward. I'm convinced even God had a good laugh at that one. I picture Him smiling as I prayed and shaking His head, knowing what was about to happen. He might have called over an angel and said, "Hey, Gabriel, get over here and watch what's about to happen to Dave! This is going to be hilarious!"

I share this silly story in a chapter about sex for a couple of reasons. First, it's funny, and you are entitled to some good laughs throughout this book. Second, even though there's nothing morally wrong about being seen naked during a medical procedure, it paints a picture of how we're not supposed to be comfortable with unrestricted nakedness around the opposite sex. I never want my boys to grow up so calloused in sin that they trade naked and unashamed with their wife for naked and shameless with a long list of casual hookups. We should never feel uncomfortable being naked in front of our spouse, but we should never feel too comfortable being naked in front of anyone who is not our spouse.

Oftentimes, the issues holding us back in the bedroom are the result of our own choices and our own mindsets. Sometimes, tragically, those issues are the result of deeper issues or other circumstances that were out of your control. We believe there should be nothing holding you back from being naked and unashamed with your spouse, and it is our hope that the stories and practical steps presented in these chapters will help you both get to the root of the issues, so you can experience God's best in your marriage. God wants your sex life within marriage to be absolutely amazing!

Questions to Consider:

1. When you think about sex, does it make you feel uncomfortable? If so, why?

2. How did your parents talk to you about sex?

3. What/who has influenced your thoughts and feelings about sex the most?

If you are not sure how to answer these questions, pray about it and ask God to reveal the truth to you. Then, talk about it with each other without making judgments or getting offended. Be an open, honest, and safe place for one another. Be willing to talk and eager to listen.

CHAPTER 2

WE ALL HAVE BAGGAGE

Misty and Jake grew up in the same church youth group. They didn't date each other at the time, but they developed a friendship that would eventually blossom into a romance when they reconnected after college. In the five years between high school graduation and their first date with each other, they both had accumulated some counterfeit climaxes and sexual baggage.

Back in their youth group days, they had been taught some of the lessons of what has since been dubbed "Purity Culture." This movement within Christianity aimed at keeping young people sexually pure and reserving all forms of sexual activity for marriage. Some of its lessons included a hyperfocus on what young people should watch on TV, how they should dress, how they should interact with the opposite sex, and how dating itself was problematic and possibly even sinful (even without sex). While the original goals of the movement were Biblical and healthy, some of the unintended consequences of its methods left a generation of church kids with confusion, insecurity, and shame related to sex (even if they had remained virgins).

Misty and Jake left their youth group and went off to separate colleges with their chastity intact and with a firm commitment to remain baggage-free virgins until marriage. Misty landed at a small Christian college where she began dating a guy who was a couple years older. A year into their relationship, she had already crossed many of the boundaries she had promised herself she'd never cross before marriage. Her boyfriend was always willing to go as far as she was comfortable going, even pushing her to go a little further.

Misty loved him and was convinced that they were going to get married. It seemed impractical to get married anytime soon, and it also seemed impossible to keep fighting the constant sexual temptation. She was sure she was with "The One," so in a heated make-out session one night in her dorm room, she and her boyfriend had sex.

It all happened so fast she could barely believe they'd actually done it. She'd built it up so much in her head that it all felt so anticlimactic and waves of guilt and shame started washing over her. Her boyfriend's response was different. He had been hoping for this moment for a long time, and now that they'd finally done it, he was convinced his sexual frustration was finally over, and they'd be doing it every day.

Misty was riding an emotional roller coaster on the days that followed. She felt a strong bond to her boyfriend and a desire to keep having sex, but she also felt dirty and ashamed that she had failed on what she'd believed to be the single most important commitment of her life. She wasn't sure what to feel or what to do.

Misty told her boyfriend that she loved him and wanted to be with him forever, but they had made a mistake and shouldn't have sex anymore. He reluctantly agreed, but it quickly became clear that he wasn't willing to stop pursuing her sexually. When she would deny him, she sensed he was pulling away, and she feared he might leave her for good. She would end up compromising and having sex as a way to keep him. This put her in a cycle of shame and insecurity where she hated herself for having sex, but she also hated the idea of losing the man she wanted to marry.

She made a mental compromise with herself to help her justify her actions. She was going to keep having sex to keep him, but she convinced herself that she wasn't allowed to enjoy it. She had to punish herself for her sin by living with the guilt and shame. She found herself resenting her boyfriend, who seemed to want sex more and more and seemed to have no regrets or baggage at all. She started to feel used and unloved, which made her guilt and shame even worse.

The peak of her emotional crisis came when in a moment of horror just days before the start of her college's Christmas break, she realized she was a week late for her period. She bought a cheap pregnancy test and felt physically ill as she waited on the results. When she looked down at the pregnancy test and saw two lines that indicated that she was pregnant, she nearly threw up.

The next couple days were among the very darkest of her life, as she tried to decide how to tell her boyfriend and her parents. She felt trapped. She had once held up signs at a Pro-Life rally, but now she found herself seriously considering getting an abortion.

Before she could muster up the courage to tell anyone she was pregnant, she started having sharp stomach pains and a heavy flow of blood. As the blood flowed, so did waves of both relief and shame. She was so relieved she wasn't pregnant, but she was ashamed of herself for getting in this position and seriously considering an abortion. She felt guilty for feeling relieved. She decided to pretend the whole ordeal never happened, and she didn't tell her boyfriend about it.

The relationship limped along for another year on autopilot, but, eventually, her boyfriend lost interest and broke up with her. She didn't know whether to feel devastated or happy. She spent the rest of her college days wrapped up in her studies, too jaded to pursue any other romantic relationships and too ashamed to wholeheartedly pursue her relationship with God. Melancholy became her default mood, and the once joyful and carefree girl grew numb.

Several hundred miles away, Jake was at a large state university. He was living in the constant tension of trying to enjoy the fun and freedom of college life while still holding onto the values he had learned at church. He had one foot in both worlds. He went to church on Sundays and was even part of young men's Bible Study on Tuesday mornings, but he also partied pretty hard on the weekends and started making all sorts of unhealthy choices in his relationships.

Jake had been exposed to pornography as a young teen, and while he'd done his best to stay away from it through most of high school, the freedom of college life and the constant temptation of his smartphone proved to be too strong a temptation.

He fell back into porn, and it quickly became an addiction. He was in a toxic cycle of binging on porn and then masturbating to the porn-fueled fantasies in his mind.

Without realizing it, Jake had evolved from a young man who had once been a great respecter of all girls and women to a guy who objectified every woman who walked by. Those fantasies didn't stay confined to his mind for long. Soon, he was hooking up with girls and acting out some of those fantasies in his dorm room. He somehow kept himself from having actual intercourse, but he was willing to do everything and anything else.

In his warped view of thinking, Jake was actually praising himself for his restraint and technical virginity. It didn't seem to register with him that his mind and actions were treating all women as sexual objects. He would sometimes feel pangs of guilt over his lifestyle, and he would pray sincere prayers of repentance, but, eventually, he would always find himself falling right back into the same old habits. He felt powerless to fight it, and, eventually, he just stopped trying.

The year after graduation, Jake and Misty reconnected on social media. There was an instant spark. They realized they had a lot of common interests, and their old friendship quickly blossomed into a new romance. As their relationship grew more serious, they both shared some of their past mistakes and began talking about marriage. They both wanted to start their marriage right, so they decided not to have sex until their wedding night.

During their relatively quick period of dating and engagement, they started to experience insecurities related to each other's past experiences. Jake was disappointed he wasn't marrying a virgin. He couldn't get past the thought of someone else having sex with the woman he was going to marry. He had prayed for a virgin bride and thought he deserved it. He harbored some resentment toward God and toward Misty over the fact that she had been deflowered by someone else. He would make comments about this in a way that made Misty feel insecure and disrespected.

Misty was also feeling insecure because of Jake's sexual experiences. Although he had never had intercourse, he'd had many encounters of a sexual nature with different young women, and he'd even seen everything imaginable through pornography. She felt simultaneously insecure that he would be comparing her to these other women and images of airbrushed bodies on a screen, and she felt disgusted he had chosen to fill his mind with such filth.

Other than these issues, their relationship seemed to be great. They were going to church together. Their faith was growing. They were getting established in their careers. They laughed a lot, and life seemed to be moving in the right direction. They were wildly attracted to each other, but they were still able to maintain their boundaries and their commitment to not having sex before the wedding. Both sets of parents thought the young couple was a great match, and there was much celebrating when the community gathered together to celebrate their wedding day.

The tropical honeymoon was amazing. It felt like a week of paradise. Whatever insecurities or baggage they may have had seemed to disappear in the distance like a Caribbean sunset. Their moments of blissful intimacy led them to believe their life together was going to feel like a never-ending honeymoon. There were even moments when Misty dared to believe that the joyful, carefree version of herself might not be gone after all.

They got back home and started settling into everyday life as a newlywed couple. They enjoyed the process of setting up their home and figuring out their new routines. Those early days were filled with a lot of flirtation, spontaneous sex, laughter, and fun. The first month of their marriage was even better than they had dreamed it would be.

Unfortunately, the honeymoon bliss didn't last forever. A few months into their marriage, the rigors of everyday life had chased away their newlywed playfulness. Stress over bills, chores, in-laws, and a myriad of other issues started overwhelming them. In his stress, Jake wanted to have even more sex. For him, sex was a form of stress relief. Misty, however, started pulling away.

For Misty, the honeymoon phase had temporarily made her forget her insecurities and baggage related to sex. Now that real life had started to settle in, she found herself dreading sex. She felt once more like that insecure college student begrudgingly giving sex to keep from losing her man, then resenting him for it. She couldn't explain what had shifted in her mind, but she no longer felt completely loved and secure in the relationship. She felt dirty and ashamed. She felt used. She started fantasizing about a life without Jake.

Jake felt frustrated. He thought they had done everything

right, and now they were going to get to a lifetime of endless sexual ecstasy. He had avoided intercourse all those years by telling himself his reward would be someday having a wife who was always eager to meet his sexual needs, but instead, his wife was becoming cold in the bedroom. He felt cheated.

It was a shock to his system, and he wasn't sure how to respond. He initially suppressed his sexual frustration and chose to treat Misty with tenderness, but it didn't take long for his angst to boil to the surface and create a sarcastic sharpness in his words. Without meaning to do it, they were both pushing each other away.

Jake fell into old habits, and he started taking care of his sexual needs on his own. While he wasn't actually looking at porn, there was a 24/7, on-demand catalog of porn clips stored in his brain anytime he wanted to access them. His daily showers started becoming suspiciously longer, and Misty soon figured out that he was masturbating every morning. For him, it was just maintenance. For her, it felt like betrayal, and she was confident that he wasn't fantasizing about her while he did it.

They still had sex occasionally. Like clockwork, every Saturday night, they would make love and then have some microwave popcorn and watch a movie in bed. It was Jake's favorite night of the week. In fact, some weeks, the thought of getting to Saturday night was the only thing that kept him going. For some reason, Misty found herself dreading it. On rare occasions, they'd have a spontaneous moment in the middle of the week, but those moments became rarer and rarer as time went on.

The marriage puttered along in an awkward state of dysfunction for several more years. Anniversaries came and went. They celebrated life's big moments, but there never seemed to be true joy or excitement in any of it. They had children and became really good at being parents, but really bad at being married. All of their tenderness and affection were reserved for their kids. They seemed to share none of it with each other. On social media, the pictures showed the images of a perfect marriage and family, but behind closed doors, they had drifted miles apart.

Baggage Check

One of our favorite Bible verses says, "Cast all your anxieties on Him, because He cares for you" (1 Peter 5:7 NIV). You can put the word "baggage" in place of the word "anxieties," and the verse's meaning is the same. Give all your baggage to Him because He cares about you. Jesus is inviting you to bring all your baggage, sin, regret, frustration, and heartbreak to Him. He loves you, and He wants to carry it for you. You were never meant to carry it yourself.

We were once at an airport checking a bag, and when we were asked to put the large suitcase up on the scale to be weighed, we were shocked at the number that came up on the screen. We had become so accustomed to rolling it around that we'd lost touch with just how heavy and cumbersome it really was. It was also really expensive because the airline's baggage fees rise with increasing weight. Traveling with heavy bags can cost you a lot more than you want to pay, both in airports and in life. This is very similar to how sexual baggage affects us. It weighs on us, and when we don't unpack it properly, it ends up costing us more than we ever thought it would. We tend to avoid talking about our own sexual baggage because we fear we will be exposed as too sexual or not sexual enough. Talking about it makes us feel vulnerable, and we live in a culture that often frowns on vulnerability. However, breakthrough requires vulnerability. God wants us to bring our burdens to him. He doesn't want us to live with the baggage of sexual shame from promiscuity, abuse, misconceptions, or backward ideologies. He wants us to live in freedom and alignment with him in all aspects of our lives.

The Apostle Paul addressed the binding power of sex all throughout 1 Corinthians because, at the time, sexual immorality was rampant in the Corinthian culture, even among the new Christians there. Paul could see the great damage it was causing, and he wanted to help them to understand the boundaries that God placed around sex. In 1 Corinthians 6:18–20, Paul says, "Flee from sexual immorality. Every other sin a person commits is outside the body, but the sexually immoral person sins against his own body. Or do you not know that your body is a temple of the Holy Spirit within you, whom you have from God? You are not your own, for you were bought with a price. So, glorify God in your body" (ESV). God designed sex to be a physical, spiritual, and emotional act to reflect the outpouring of love a husband and wife feel for each other. It is also a consummative act that represents the lifelong covenant that they are making with one another. Sex is designed to be binding and weighty, and that is what Paul was trying to help the Corinthians to understand. The

Corinthians were carrying around loads of sexual baggage, like so many of us are today, and it all stemmed from their skewed mindsets about sex, much like our current cultural context. We also must often push against the current to shed the weight of our own sexual baggage, but we can do it with God's help.

> God designed sex to be a physical, spiritual, and emotional act to reflect the outpouring of love a husband and wife feel for each other.

In the next chapter, we will talk more specifically about how you and your spouse can identify and unpack the lies that have led you to your sexual baggage; however, we hope that you take a look at the questions at the end of this chapter and discuss them together. We can't shed our sexual baggage without being honest and vulnerable about it with ourselves *and* with our spouses. It might be an awkward conversation at first, but again, we must be willing to push against the current to experience real breakthrough.

Jake and Misty spent years carrying around heavy baggage without ever acknowledging that they were carrying it. They let their marriage get to a crisis point before they started taking steps to address it. They eventually went to counseling which led to a lot of healing, but so much damage could have been prevented if they'd been proactive and started the healing process sooner. We believe it's never too late to work on your marriage, but it's also never too early. A healthy marriage needs consistent attention, investment, and self-assessment. We can easily slip into autopilot where everything seems "fine," but if those consistent investments aren't being made, it can trigger unexpected turbulence in your home.

> **We can't shed our sexual baggage without being honest and vulnerable about it with ourselves and with our spouses.**

If you're reading this and you feel like you're already in a place of crisis, please don't lose hope! You're taking such a wise step by doing something intentional to work on yourself and your marriage. The very fact that you're reading this book right now shows that you're a person of action who truly wants a healthy marriage. God always honors the actions we take to move toward healthier and holier living. Keep taking those healthy actions and consider talking to a Christian counselor or someone on our team at xomarriage.com/help.

If you are not in a crisis, then taking some consistent baggage-check actions will help safeguard your marriage from ever getting to a breaking point. It's good to take honest self-assessments when you're in a crisis, but it's even better to do it when things seem to be going well. Even the healthiest individuals and the happiest marriages have some baggage that could threaten to cause chaos down the road if left unchecked.

There's certainly no one-size-fits-all approach to baggage, but in one form or another, we're all carrying some. Maybe your baggage looks different from Jake and Misty's story, or perhaps, you saw a lot of yourself in their journey. The first step in dealing with sexual baggage is to identify its source. When we start doing the work of identifying the source of our baggage, we often discover it's rooted in lies we've believed. Identifying and unpacking the lies is the first step to finding freedom.

Questions to Consider:

1. Do you look forward to sex or dread it? Why?

2. When you and your spouse make love, do you have any thoughts that come to mind that make you feel ashamed, nervous, dirty, unfocused, or numb? If so, what are they?

CHAPTER 3

IDENTIFYING AND UNPACKING THE LIES

Married couples have been ambushed with lies that attempt to undermine God's perfect plans for them since the establishment of the very first marriage. This goes all the way back to the beginning. The very first married couple started out in perfection, but it didn't take long before a deceiver slithered into their lives and started making them doubt God's plans and motives.

The Book of Genesis in the Bible paints a beautiful picture of God's plans for Adam and Eve. He gave them everything they needed, and—for a beautiful, brief moment in time—they knew perfect intimacy with God and with each other. The Bible tells us they were both naked, but they didn't feel a hint of shame or fear. It was perfect until a serpent came into the picture and started whispering lies.

When Adam and Eve chose to trust the voice of a deceiver instead of the voice of their Heavenly Father, they sabotaged the paradise God had given them. They created drama and doubt where there had been none. They lost their perfect, naked relationship and covered themselves in shame. Insecurity replaced intimacy. We go into much more detail about this in our book, *The Naked Marriage*.

When we believe lies and counterfeit versions of love, insecurity will always replace intimacy. There's still a deceiver slithering around in our world, and his lies have become even more crafty and insidious. Whenever we lose sight of God's truth, we're opening ourselves up to be deceived. That's what happened to Shawn and Madison.

> **When we believe lies and counterfeit versions of love, insecurity will always replace intimacy.**

The two future lovebirds met in a CrossFit class where they both excelled and pushed themselves to the limit. They were instantly drawn to each other's intensity and discipline. They were probably also drawn to each other's abs. (For the record, neither of us have ever had chiseled abs. We've always loved chips and guacamole more than we've loved doing crunches, but this story isn't about our lack of abs. This is about Shawn and Madison.)

After catching each other's eyes from across the room, they connected after class one night and immediately struck up a conversation. There was an instant connection. They were not only drawn to each other physically, but intellectually as well. It was a Tuesday night, and they both had early starts the next day, but they decided to go out for drinks.

They talked late into the night and couldn't believe they'd been there for three hours when the bartender yelled out it was time for last call. They hadn't planned to be out drinking and laughing until midnight, but there they were.

They both felt fine to drive, but Madison said, "Let's not taking any chances on getting a DUI. Let's get an Uber."

Shawn smiled slyly and said, "One Uber or two?"

She laughed and bit her lower lip with a flirtatious look in her eye. "You can crash at my place."

The sexual tension was so strong in the backseat of that car they barely made it through the front door of Madison's apartment before they started undressing each other. There was a moment of awkwardness the next morning when they woke up naked and sober, unsure of how to proceed in this unexpected situation. Madison broke the ice when she snuggled up next to Shawn, and within a few moments, they were rolling around the bed again.

Their one-night stand quickly evolved into a full-fledged relationship. They moved in together a few months later, and a year after that, they were standing on a beach surrounded by a small group of family and friends to exchange their vows. They looked like models on the cover of a magazine as they kissed with the sun setting over the ocean behind them.

Within their first year of marriage, as it usually does, a lot started coming to the surface. Issues they had both kept relatively hidden before marriage were now beginning to emerge. There was fighting, insecurities, secrets, and all kinds of unhealthy communication. Things were tumultuous at home, and they seemed to be getting worse by the day.

They might have been headed for divorce before they reached their first anniversary had it not been for a surprise pregnancy. The birth of their daughter united them together in a way neither of them expected. As long as their primary focus remained on their little girl, their relationship with each other seemed sustainable.

They continued on in the fitness world, eventually opening up a gym together. They were accomplished trainers and business partners. Their gym and their precious little girl were the highlights of their world, but their marriage was never the primary focus. They'd both grown up in homes where they hadn't seen great examples of marriage, so they really didn't even know theirs wasn't healthy.

About a decade into their marriage, Madison started feeling insecure about her body. She didn't want any additional kids because of the toll the first pregnancy took on her figure, but now the combination of age, stress, and motherhood was making it impossible for her to maintain her once flawless physique. Shawn had never put any pressure on her to maintain a certain weight or figure, but her insecurities soon manifested as outbursts of jealousy.

Madison would lose it on Shawn if she thought he was checking out another woman in the gym. He would reassure her that he only had eyes for her, but she was still always accusing him. Even if it was purely work-related, if he had to have a conversation with another woman and she found out about it, she would yell and cuss at him. Her jealousy was relentless, and Shawn wasn't sure how to address it and reassure her of his love and commitment to her.

Shawn was never offended by her jealousy. In fact, he seemed to almost enjoy Madison's infatuation with him. It made him feel loved. Sometimes, he'd even linger next to an attractive girl and wait for Madison to walk by just so he could get a reaction from her. He himself was never the jealous type, but he did have a temper. He had once knocked a guy out in a bar fight just because the guy made fun of his haircut. Shawn swore his angry days were behind him, but it always seemed to have some control over him.

Other than a few angry outbursts over the years which had really scared Madison, he had managed to suppress it for the most part. For reasons he couldn't fully explain, his fuse had become shorter and shorter lately. He was having a harder time controlling it. Whenever Madison would offer suggestions about what he should do or what he should eat or wear, he would snap at her in an aggressive way. He had been tender and patient toward her for most of their dating relationship, but now anger seemed to always boil right below the surface. She walked on eggshells around their house because she never knew what would trigger him.

All those years, Madison and Shawn were both unaware of the lies they believed about themselves and each other. Madison hadn't shared with Shawn that she secretly dealt with feelings of inferiority, and she had always felt like she was unattractive and undesirable. Madison's dad had always talked about how beautiful her sister was, but he never talked about her like that. She was a chubby and awkward little girl, and her dad would often make fun of her belly. Madison assumed her dad was probably trying to help her want to lose weight, but it just made her feel worse. Many times, she would end up turning to junk food to ease the pain and embarrassment.

In her formative years, Madison believed the lie that she was ugly and undesirable. In response to that lie, she became obsessed with working out and becoming physically strong, and slowly but surely, her body began to change. Madison didn't know how to handle the newfound attention she received from men, but she knew that she liked it. So, in her late teens and early twenties, she became sexually aggressive and promiscuous. She even developed a secret eating disorder as a teenager that continued into adulthood. Even at the peak of physical fitness, she still looked in the mirror and saw herself as fat and undesirable. In her insecurity, she was constantly reaching out to men for their approval of her appearance.

After she married Shawn, Madison still dressed in provocative ways, not just for Shawn, but to turn the heads of other men. She wasn't doing it for sex. She was doing it for approval. It was as if every time a man noticed her, the voice of that chubby little girl inside of her was shouting, "Look, Daddy! Do you see? I am pretty! I'm not the ugly daughter anymore. I'm desirable. I'm wanted."

Madison's fierce anger toward Shawn whenever he would talk to another woman at work was rooted in this same lie. The thought of her husband even noticing other women made her feel like that insecure little girl again. His words of reassurance meant nothing to her because his voice wasn't nearly as convincing as the voice that had been in her own head since she was a little girl. This core lie had sabotaged Madison's thinking and her self-image for so long. This lie had led her to some reckless behaviors and shallow relationships, and deep down, she knew something had to change. Through Christian therapy, Madison was able to identify this lie and replace it with

God's truth that she is His masterpiece (Ephesians 2:10) and His precious daughter (Romans 8:14-15) who is "fearfully and wonderfully made" (Psalm 139:14 NIV). It was a process, but over time, Madison believed these truths and fully accepted and embraced herself as the beautiful human being that she is, both inside and out.

Shawn was also struggling with some lies of his own. His biological dad was never really in the picture when he was growing up. His mom and dad never married each other, and his dad left before he was even born. It was just Shawn and his mom until he was in kindergarten, and then his mom met his soon-to-be stepdad. Shawn always felt like his stepdad seemed embarrassed by him because Shawn was biracial, whereas his mom and stepdad were white. So, Shawn stuck out a little, and it made him feel unloved. When his mom and stepdad started having kids of their own, Shawn's feelings of not having a place in the family were accentuated. His mom and stepdad stopped including Shawn in all of their family activities, and he was left alone at home quite a bit. His mom's "new family" seemed to take up all of her time. When he'd try to talk to her about his feelings, she'd seem exasperated and ask him if they could talk later, but they rarely did.

In desperation, Shawn would go to his stepdad for advice only to be turned away with an, "I'm too busy for this" or "Can't you just figure this out on your own?" His biological dad only seemed to come around when he needed something from Shawn, like money or a ride. He was more like Shawn's child than his parent. Deep in his heart, Shawn felt like he had two different dads who didn't love him, so he assumed that he must be unlovable. His family went to church, but when they talked about God as a Father, Shawn immediately assumed that God couldn't really love him either.

When Shawn was corrected by his parents, it wasn't done in a loving way. He felt cast aside and abandoned. This feeling followed him into adulthood, and Shawn turned to working out and building muscle as a means to push the feeling away. He figured that if he couldn't have love, he'd settle for respect or even for fear. He just didn't want to feel powerless anymore. His powerful persona seemed to get him the respect he wanted to the point where he didn't even think he needed to feel loved anymore. "Respect is what I really need," he'd tell himself. That was until he married Madison, and she began to bring up concerns about their relationship or his behavior. Shawn couldn't take it. Even when she tried to bring rather small concerns to his attention, Shawn felt attacked and disrespected, like the powerless, unloved kid that he used to be. He feared Madison would leave him like everyone else had in his life, even though she'd never done anything to break his trust and had always been there for him.

At a very young age, Shawn believed two lies: *1. I am unlovable. 2. Everyone leaves.* Through Christian counseling, Shawn gradually unpacked these two lies and replaced them with God's truth that he is worthy of love (Isaiah 43:4) and loved by God (John 3:16). He also realized that he wasn't fully trusting Madison because he felt like he could never depend on his parents to be there for him. Madison had never abandoned him, and he recognized that he was sabotaging their relationship by refusing to trust her. Over time, Shawn was able to forgive his parents and lay down the resentment and hurt he had been holding onto all those years. He stopped trying to ward people off with intimidation and began to assume the best in people instead of automatically assuming the worst.

Both Shawn and Madison committed to work even harder on the health of their marriage than they had always worked on the health of their bodies, and a year later, they decided to have another baby. Madison's previous fear of pregnancy had always infringed on her ability to enjoy sex, but after unpacking the lies she'd believed about her worth being tied to her appearance, she was excited at the prospect of pregnancy once again. She was finally at peace. For her, being a wife and mom was far more important than having visible abs and no stretch marks. Shawn also let go of some of what he'd been holding onto as part of his identity. He had stepped away from the gym, and while he still worked out occasionally, he had visible love handles for the first time in his life. Madison actually loved his new *dad bod*. Knowing that Madison respected and loved him regardless of his level of strength and prowess at that moment made him fall even deeper in love with her, and they both experienced a depth of passion and intimacy they never thought possible.

Shawn and Madison did the work, took the time, and made the commitment to unlearn the lies they'd believed for so long while being patient with themselves and each other along the way. They still have struggles like all couples do, but they're finally facing their struggles in a unified and healthy way, and that's what makes all the difference. They're finally united and moving in the right direction together—free from the baggage of their pasts.

The Lies that Make People Leave

Shawn and Madison were willing to do the work, but every couple must make that decision for themselves. There will be times in your marriage when you're tempted to believe the lies, and giving up on your marriage will seem like the best option. It might even seem like the only option. In those moments, we want you to remember that there's still hope. This is a truth we've seen play out time and time again with people who were on the fence about whether they should stay in their marriage or call it quits. Maybe you believe some of the lies that Madison and Shawn believed, or maybe you believe some other lies. Here are some common lies that make people leave:

1. "We've just fallen out of love."

When our marriage is in a tough spot, it can feel like all love has been lost. The passion wanes, sex becomes nonexistent, molehills become mountains, and our emotions quickly go from weary to numb. However, we must remember that real, lasting love is much more about commitment and much less about our feelings. In fact, feelings are fickle. They are meant to be a signal, not a compass. Feelings are symptoms of our cognitive processing; they are not designed to be our guide. In 1 Corinthians 13:4–5, Paul states, "Love is patient, love is kind.

> **Real, lasting love is much more about commitment and much less about our feelings. In fact, feelings are fickle. They are meant to be a signal, not a compass.**

It does not envy, it does not boast, it is not proud. It does not dishonor others, it is not self-seeking, it is not easily angered, it keeps no record of wrongs" (NIV). That's not a wishy-washy, tepid kind of love. That's the kind of love that lasts forever. Paul goes on to say that love "always protects, always trusts, always hopes, always perseveres" (v. 7). When life is hard and our relationship seems to be more difficult than usual, our feelings will change, but our commitment can be unwavering when we *choose* to stay committed through thick and thin. We can't necessarily choose our feelings all the time. We're human. However, we can choose to love our spouse enough to stay committed to them. There is nothing sexier than a man or woman who is fully committed to their spouse—mind, body, and soul.

2. "I'm just not physically attracted to my spouse anymore."

This is a tough one, and sadly, it is one of the most damaging lies spouses believe. Attraction is important, and physical and/ or sexual attraction is often one of the first things that draws us to our spouse. However, chemistry alone can't sustain a marriage. Still, we are human. We long to *feel* attraction and sexual energy toward our spouse, and we want to see the desire they have for us in their eyes and body language. However, the truth is, every couple goes through dry periods where the flame of desire is barely flickering due to the realities of life—busy work schedules, running kids to and from activities, health challenges, taking care of aging parents, etc. Life can be exhausting at times, and we can easily put our bodies and our relationship on the back burner. However, we must intentionally fight against this negative tendency. It starts with us individually focusing on what we can do to stay physically healthy instead of being critical of our spouse's body. We also need to remember that the longest-lasting form of attraction is on a soul level. Real beauty radiates from the heart even when wrinkles settle in, and muscle definition is less visible. We will experience the best sex we've ever had with our spouse when we see them as more than just a body to be positioned to meet our sexual needs. Sex is a holy marital act—a conjoining of two minds, two bodies, and two souls—and an exclusive experience that God designed for married couples to celebrate their love and commitment in a deeply climactic and pleasurable way, to further connect a husband and wife on a soul level.

Don't believe the lie that you've lost your desire for your spouse. Instead, think about what first drew you to them on a soul level. Was it the way she loved her family? Was it the way he showed loyalty to his friends? Was it how she encouraged you in hard times? Was it how he challenged you to grow deeper in your walk with the Lord? What attracts you to your spouse on a soul level? After you think about these things, talk to your spouse about them and thank them for these things. This will draw you closer together and ward off this lie.

3. "He or she just can't give me what I need."

A spouse has the power to lift our spirits with encouragement or bring us down with harsh criticism. We should all be aiming for the former. When it comes to sex, our spouse can bring us to the heights of passion or make us feel like our marriage bed is a lonely, cold place. Again, we should aim for the former. When we become hyperfocused on how our own needs aren't being met, we can inadvertently disregard the fact that we might be failing to meet our spouse's needs as well. That is why communication is key. If you feel your spouse isn't treating you right or doesn't prioritize sex the way you'd like them to, then you must address these issues with them in the most direct but loving way possible. The most effective way to start these conversations is by asking your spouse if there is anything they need from *you*. This defuses the tension and allows you to gain insight into how you can serve your spouse as well. Be sure to listen intently to your spouse's answer and be willing to make any necessary changes. After this, be honest about what you'd like your spouse to do better in meeting your needs. If they get tense, tell your spouse what they are already doing right in meeting your needs, thank them, and then remind them that you are just trying to be honest and open with them.

Don't have this conversation in the heat of an argument or in the act of making love. That won't go well. Have these conversations when both of you are able to talk and listen well with clear heads.

You might be reading this thinking, *Well, that's never going to happen! We are never both in good moods and ready to talk!* Listen, the conditions don't have to be perfect to have a healthy conversation; however, it does require one of you to take the first courageous step to open up and get real about your marriage. Truth is, your spouse will never be able to give you what you need if they don't understand what your needs are and vice versa. However, sometimes, we can find ourselves looking to our spouse to fulfill our deepest need—a God-sized void in our hearts.

If you feel you lack something in your heart, please don't look to your spouse to fill it. Yes, we need love, support, and sexual fulfillment regularly from our spouse, and we should do our best to serve our spouse in those ways as much as we can as well. Still, they do not have the power to make us whole. Jesus does. God made you. He knows you, and He wants you to know Him. He wants to bring you a wholeness that only He can provide. When you fully surrender and accept the amazing gift of forgiveness that God has given us through the death and resurrection of His one and only Son, Jesus Christ, you will finally find the wholeness you have been searching for. This doesn't mean you will never feel lonely or sad, but it does mean you have a relationship with your Maker—the One who knows how to truly heal your scars. He is the One who completes you.

4. "If we were meant to stay married, then it wouldn't be this hard."

Every marriage goes through ups and downs. That's precisely why we say vows like "…for better or for worse…" We relish the good days, but what are we supposed to do when we feel

> **The conditions don't have to be perfect to have a healthy conversation; however, it does require one of you to take the first courageous step to open up and get real about your marriage.**

stuck in a prolonged "for worse" season—when we feel like we are trying our best, but our circumstances and feelings keep getting in the way of our progress? I believe these are the moments when the enemy likes to attack our marriage the most. He comes on strong when our defenses are down and we are exhausted and dismayed. Make no mistake, he is out to get us. Satan is a thief who only comes to steal, kill, and destroy (John 10:10), and he would love nothing more than to break up our marriage and family.

None of us are immune to hardship in life, but every one of us has the power to choose how we react to it. It's easy to be a good husband or wife when things seem to be going well, but what about when things get hard? How should we handle a cancer diagnosis, the death of a loved one, financial hardship, job issues, moving, bad decisions, sexual issues, and other crises? What are we supposed to do when we are under attack? How do we fight the enemy? We keep talking to one another (Colossians 4:6), we try to inspire the changes we'd like to see in our spouse (James 3:18), we pray for our spouse (Psalm 66:20), we prioritize spending more time together (Hebrews 10:25a), and we cling to the Lord's promises and remain patient with the process of healing refinement (Psalm 12:6).

Don't believe this lie! You and your spouse can get through this season. When you choose to reconnect with your spouse and check back into your marriage, your marriage will become even stronger. Choose to fight for each other, not against one another. We serve a God who still brings dead things to life, and that includes a worn-out, lifeless marriage (Romans 4:17). Our Father can bring healing to our mess. He can breathe new life into our relationship and make it more beautiful, more life-giving, more intimate, and more trusting than we ever thought possible (Isaiah 61:3). But, we can't be complacent and let the enemy continue to attack us.

WE. MUST. FIGHT. BACK.

5. "I'd be better off alone. I don't really need him or her anymore."

This lie is one of the most prevalent ones. Our culture has perpetuated this lie and tried to convince us that needing our spouse is a sign of personal weakness, that it makes us "needy" or gives our spouse too much power in our life. However, a marriage will quickly become a lonely place unless both spouses are willing to lean on each other and care for one another as God intended. We don't give up our individuality when we marry, but we do choose to trade our completely independent lives for a supportive, interdependent union with our spouses. A healthy, balanced marriage is like a beautiful ballroom dance where the husband and wife are completely intertwined and in tune with one another, with God leading them in their journey together.

When we marry, we become one with our spouse—physically, mentally, emotionally, and spiritually. Physical oneness through sex is often the most celebrated and enjoyed part of marriage for most couples in the early years of their marriage. However, the rise in self-satisfying sexual fulfillment practices, such as porn and masturbation, have perpetuated this lie even further. Porn is rampant in the world, even among Christians, and it is wreaking havoc on marriages. The porn-addicted often feel helpless to stop, and the habit of fantasy-fueled masturbation dies hard. However, there is hope in stopping these toxic habits and cultivating a deeply satisfying, connected sex life with your spouse. We don't have to live with the baggage of shame, regret, disillusionment, constant temptation, and raging unmet sexual needs that come with porn and masturbation. We can be free from it. The first step is identifying and unpacking the *lie* that meeting your sexual needs on your own, however you see fit, is harmless to you and your spouse.

Questions to Consider:

1. What lies do you believe about yourself, your spouse, and your marriage?

2. How do these lies negatively affect you, how your treat your spouse, and the state of your marriage?

3. What truths can replace these lies in your mindset?

4. How would focusing on these truths change your marriage for the better?

CHAPTER 4

THE PORN ERA

If there's one force in our world causing more relational bag-gage and broken views about sex, that toxic force would be pornography. In the work we do, we receive messages every single day from individuals and couples whose lives have been negatively impacted by porn. Porn's cultural influence impacts us all, even if you're not currently consuming it. Porn is the very definition of a counterfeit climax.

The Bible uses graphic language to describe the dangers of giving in to lust. One of the most sexually graphic passages from the Bible can be found in Ezekiel 23, where the prophet uses the imagery of sexual promiscuity and lust to represent the spiritual idolatry happening in the nation of Israel. Within the broader passage, one eye-opening verse says, "She lusted after lovers with genitals as large as a donkey's and emissions like those of a horse" (Ezekiel 23:20). And you thought the Bible was boring!

This graphic verse and others like it give a stark warning about the twin sins of idolatry and lust. Idolatry is misusing your soul by looking for spiritual fulfillment in anything other than God. Lust is misusing your body (and the bodies of oth-ers) by seeking sexual pleasure anywhere outside of marriage. In our culture, pornography has become the new idol sabotag-ing both the bodies and souls of those who consume it.

Another aspect of this graphic verse is that it describes sexual lust in animalistic terms. Porn creates an artificial intimacy that dehumanizes both the consumer and the actors on the screen. It portrays human beings as bodies to be used in animalistic, temporary pleasure without ever acknowledging their sacred, eternal soul. It feeds our lust, which leads us down a dark road toward a poisoned mind, an addicted body, and a numbed soul.

> **Porn creates an artificial intimacy that dehumanizes both the consumer and the actors on the screen.**

Fully understanding the dangers and ubiquitous influence of porn is one of the most effective ways to safeguard your mind and your marriage. Even if porn isn't currently an issue for you, or if you don't think there's anything at all wrong with viewing porn, please stick with us, and don't skip over this chapter. This might prove the be the most eye-opening moment in the entire book for you.

My (Dave's) own struggle with pornography began as an adolescent curiosity. Nearly all boys are stimulated by visual images of females, and once the testosterone starts to kick in, the temptation to look and lust can become overwhelming. In my younger years, the options for lusting were limited. It was practically the Dark Ages when I was in middle school, so the Internet wasn't accessible. My first memories of intentional lust happened at Walmart. Yes, you heard that right: Walmart. I know, I know, it's sad.

Walmart had a section where you could look through posters. The posters were in frames and connected to a plastic, rotating spine that allowed you to flip through them one at a time as if you were turning the pages on a giant book. The posters were mostly innocent. There were posters of cartoons and baseball players and fast cars but hidden away in the middle, there was always at least one poster of a girl in a bikini.

When we'd get to Walmart, I'd always tell Mom I wanted to go look around. I'd break loose from the family pack and make a beeline for the posters. I'd wait until nobody else was around, and then I'd go through the routine of pretending to look at all the posters when really, I was just fixating on the bikini girl.

My curiosity with bikinis quickly morphed into a curiosity of women without bikinis. I had a friend who had some *Playboy* magazines under his bed. I remember the first time he handed me one. It felt like fire burning in my hands. My heart was racing. I knew it was wrong to lust after women, but all the willpower I could summon wasn't nearly enough to keep me from opening up that centerfold. Once I saw those airbrushed images, I was hooked, but being hooked on porn doesn't mean you want more of the same thing. It means you always need something different.

Then, one of my friends got ahold of some hardcore porn magazines. Once I saw those graphic images, looking wasn't enough anymore. I had to have a physical release while I looked. Those magazines pierced me with the double-edged sword of porn and masturbation. I'd look, and then I'd fantasize, and then I'd masturbate.

The magazines paved the way to movies, and, by this time, Internet access to porn made every fantasy just a click away.

My brain was being rewired to see women as sexual objects there for my on-demand access, to use and discard at my disposal. I was losing control. Even when I was able to go stretches of time without looking at porn, I'd still replay those images in my mind and masturbate daily. It was an addictive cycle, and I wasn't sure I'd ever break free.

I justified in my mind that I wasn't really using anyone since these were merely images on a screen or in a magazine. This was just entertainment. Nobody was getting hurt. I believed that lie for a while until I noticed that I could no longer look at an attractive woman without undressing her in my mind and fantasizing about her performing sexual acts at my command.

My mind became a warped place. My lustful sins had sabotaged my good intentions, and I'd lost control. By sheer willpower, I'd stay away from porn for weeks or even months at a time, but I'd always fall back into that same dark pit because I never sought accountability. I never followed the biblical roadmap for healing, which always involves repentance. I followed the path of pride, and pride tells you that nobody needs to know, and you can take care of things on your own.

I carried my porn secret into my marriage without telling Ashley it had been a past struggle. I thought I had been "cured" of it, and I also believed the myth that once I was married and had a healthy outlet for my sex drive, I'd never be tempted by porn

> **I also believed the myth that once I was married and had a healthy outlet for my sex drive, I'd never be tempted by porn again.**

again. I turned out to be very wrong, and I fell back into that same dark pit about a year into our marriage.

When Ashley found the sites I'd visited on our computer, I was heartbroken, ashamed, and relieved all at once. We started a journey toward healing, and I'm so thankful she responded with grace. Even though she was deeply wounded by my dishonesty and my lustful sin, she chose to forgive and offered me the opportunity to rebuild the trust I'd broken.

I'm so thankful for God's grace and for my wife's grace. I don't know where I'd be without them! I'm happy to report that I've been free from porn for years now. While it seems like a distant memory, I still battle against the dark images embedded in my mind and I still find myself having to pry my eyes away from seductive images all around me. It's an ongoing battle for me and for most men of all ages (and a growing number of women too).

Every stat I've seen says that the majority of men have a current struggle with porn, but porn isn't just a male issue. For an ever-growing percentage of women, porn has

> **We can't expect our words of respect to be believed when our eyes are telling a different story. We must be a generation that agrees with Jesus that lust is sin.**

become an addiction. I see that familiar look in the eyes of so many. It's a look I used to have, and I still battle against. It's a look of scanning the horizon looking for anyone to "check out." It's a look that objectifies, mentally undresses, and uses people instead of respecting them.

We can't expect our words of respect to be believed when our eyes are telling a different story. We must be a generation that agrees with Jesus that lust is sin. Porn is immeasurably harmful to both the actors who make it and the billions of consumers who watch it.

The Truth About Women and Porn

Let's face it. We are all visual creatures, and nudity draws us in like flies to a bright light. This really isn't a bad thing. In fact, God made human beings this way on purpose. He made us sexual so we could experience intimate pleasure with our spouse and possibly have children one day. We are supposed to appreciate the naked body. We are wired to desire sex. It isn't gross; it's beautiful. Unfortunately, our culture often represents it as everything but the amazing gift that it is.

I (Ashley) recently watched part of an episode of a reality show that follows the glamorous lives of several famous married women. You might know what show I'm referring to, and it can be addicting to watch. During this particular show, one housewife was discussing what she described as the secret to her then-seventeen-year marriage. She said they both "worked at it" and did things to "spice things up," including watching porn together on a regular basis. She then commented that most of her friends didn't watch porn with their spouses, and she thinks that everyone would have better marriages if they watched it together. I honestly couldn't believe how comfortable she was in admitting that this was a regular practice in her marriage. Even if it were true, most people wouldn't admit to it on national television. She was not only admitting it; she was celebrating it and even advising it. I couldn't help but ask myself, "Is porn really becoming this socially acceptable?"

The more I've thought about and now researched this, I've realized that this famous housewife's view of porn is increasingly becoming commonplace. Lots of people are watching it, and it's not just men. Statistics show that more and more women are paying for porn today. Porn has certainly permeated our society, but it's not just through the porn industry itself, even though their reported profits are astonishingly high.

Unless you are living completely off the grid, you may have heard of a little book called, *Fifty Shades of Grey* and multiple box office smash hit movies based on the book series. I'll be honest, I've never read *Fifty Shades,* but I have talked with many friends and family members who have. I've also seen parts of the movies edited for and played on television. It's racy, to say the least. Please don't misunderstand me, friend. If you are not a Christian, I don't see any reason why you didn't read the books or watch the movies. Who wouldn't want to read about an extremely good-looking, successful, and mysterious man who supposedly sweeps a young, innocent, and sexually inexperienced young lady right off her feet? Did I mention that it has been described as "graphic" and "a guilty pleasure"? I get it. I do. It is no wonder that more than 100 million copies have been sold worldwide, according to the *New York Times.*

However, for those of us who are Christians, we need to pause here and ask ourselves how God wants us to respond to all of this, and I am speaking to myself here. *Fifty Shades* isn't the first salacious novel or movie series to pop up in our culture, and it won't be the last. When we read novels filled with erotic scenes, our brains respond in a very similar way as if we are watching an explicit sexual act. For many women, it is all about the fantasy. That is the very reason many of us end up reading these novels. What we fail to realize is that we are opening ourselves up to lustful thinking that doesn't involve our spouse, and this is detrimental to our marriages. In Matthew 5:28, Jesus gives us a sober warning against lust when He tells us, "But I tell you that anyone who looks at a woman lustfully has already committed adultery with her in his heart" (NIV). The same goes for women looking at men lustfully. We tell ourselves it is harmless because we aren't engaging in the act with any person outside of our marriage, but Jesus clearly raises the standard for Christ followers here when He states that thinking about it is just as sinful as doing it. He doesn't tell us this to make our lives extra hard; He is trying to teach us how to guard our minds and hearts against sexual sin. As Christian wives, we are called to only have eyes and longing for our husbands. Allowing ourselves to

> **When we read novels filled with erotic scenes, our brains respond in a very similar way as if we are watching an explicit sexual act.**

be gripped by lustful thoughts that are sure to come from these seemingly harmless, sexually driven novels or movies only trains our minds and hearts to be unsatisfied with our own sex lives. It's so easy to compromise our beliefs when it comes to this. I, too, have read a little too much, looked a little too long, and pondered longer than I should have. That is exactly what lust does to us. It seems so innocent at the time, but it is an act of subtle disobedience that only leads us down a road of insecurity and emptiness, not to mention broken relationships.

Throughout our marriage ministry, Dave and I have talked to many couples contemplating divorce. When we would try to get to the root of their marital issues, the couple would often share that they had not had sex for months or even years. In many of these situations, the husband was frequently looking at porn, and the wife was filling the void with steamy romance novels, movies, and nights out with girlfriends. The couple would tell us that they'd lost interest in each other and considered themselves to be "out of love"—one of those lies that make people leave that we discussed earlier. What they failed to see was the common denominator: lust. They had stopped desiring each other, so they were seeking to fill their sexual desires elsewhere. Sometimes, these husbands and wives would end up having full-blown emotional or even physical affairs, which only made the road to healing much more difficult.

I (Ashley) am not sharing all of this to make anyone feel guilty or hopeless. God loves us and understands us. He forgives the repentant. There is always hope. I have seen husbands with a hidden porn addiction find healing and restoration for their marriages. I know wives who have turned away from a lifestyle filled with lust and a loveless marriage only to find that they can have a fulfilling marriage on all levels free from erotic novels and porn and full of God's blessings. We don't have to accept whatever our culture deems as socially acceptable. If we want our marriages to be strong, we must turn our hearts and minds to God, and He will help us to keep our eyes, minds, and hearts from wandering. He will bless all aspects of our marriages, including our sex lives. So, let's keep movie characters, empty novel fantasies, and ridiculous porn scenarios out of our bedrooms and enjoy the beautiful intimate union that we can have with our spouses. You don't need porn or some made-up steamy novel to spice up your marriage anyway.

What Every Person Needs to Know About Porn

It seems so obvious: If we invent a machine, the first thing we are going to do—after making a profit—is use it to watch porn. When the projector was invented roughly a century ago, the first movies were not of damsels in distress tied to train tracks or Charlie Chaplin–style slapsticks; they were stilted porn shorts called stag films. VHS became the standard for VCRs largely because Sony wouldn't allow pornographers to use Betamax; the movie industry followed porn's lead. DVDs, the Internet, cell phones. You name it, pornography planted its big flag there first, or at least shortly thereafter.

—Damon Brown, author of *Porn and Pong and Playboy's Greatest Covers*[2]

---

2 Damon Brown, "PCs in ecstasy: The evolution of sex in PC games," *Computer Games Magazine*, May 2006, quoted in Covenant Eyes, *Pornography Statistics*, https://www.covenanteyes.com/pornstats/.

This material is more aggressive, more harmful, more violent, more degrading and damaging than at any other time in the history of the world. And this generation growing up is dealing with it to an intensity and scale no other generation in the history of the world has ever had to.

—Clay Olsen, co-founder and CEO of Fight the New Drug[3]

We have spent years researching the dangers of porn, and, daily, we're reminded of those dangers when we see the casualties of porn in the form of broken marriages. We could write a volume of books on the topic of porn alone, but we don't want to bombard you with information. For our purposes in this chapter, we simply want to equip you with six important facts about the dangers of porn and its counterfeit messages about love and sex.

1. The average age of first exposure to pornography is twelve years old.[4] By the time a child has graduated from high school, 93% of boys and 62% of girls have been exposed to porn, whether they were looking for it or not.[5]

---

3 Shawn McDowell, Michael Leahy, and Clay Olsen, "Forum: Talking to Students," *The Set Free Global Summit*, April 6. 2016. https://vimeo.com/173068565/64df8d9e63, quoted in Covenant Eyes, *Pornography Statistics*, https://www.covenanteyes.com/pornstats/.

4 Elizabeth M. Morgan, "Association between young adults' use of sexually explicit materials and their sexual preferences, behaviors, and satisfaction," Journal of Sex Research 48 (2011): 520–530, quoted in Covenant Eyes, *Pornography Statistics*, https://www.covenanteyes.com/pornstats/.

5 Chiara Sabina, Janis Wolak, and David Finkelhor, "The nature and dynamics of Internet pornography exposure for youth," CyberPsychology and Behavior 11 (2008): 691–693, quoted in Covenant Eyes, *Pornography Statistics*, https://www.covenanteyes.com/pornstats/.

When lust goes unchecked and porn use intensifies, a young person's mind can scarcely think of a person without mentally objectifying and disrespecting her or him. I know this from research, but I also know this from personal experience. Porn producers are aggressively pushing their smut to turn people into addicted porn consumers. Some tools help you block porn and monitor all Internet activity. A few great resources to help you are Circle®, which is an Internet filtering device from Disney, as well as porn-blocking software like Covenant Eyes™ or X3Watch.

2. The actors in porn films perpetuate a fantasy, but they're often in physical pain.

Carlo Scalisi, the owner of a pornographic production company, was quoted as saying, "Amateurs come across better on screen. Our customers feel that. Especially by women you can see it. They still feel strong pain."[6] Let that thought sink in. Much of the porn industry is intentionally serving up graphic, violent content objectifying women and cultivating a twisted version of pleasure brought on by seeing a woman suffering. We're not sure how any reasonable person could think there's no link between the porn industry and our world's widespread mistreatment of women. Intentionally causing a woman pain or deriving pleasure from her pain is a grotesque form of disrespect.

---

6 Katharine Sarikakis and Zeenia Shaukat, "The global structures and cultures of pornography: The global brothel," in Feminist Interventions in International Communications: Minding the Gap, ed. Katharine Sarikakis and Leslie Regan Shade (Plymouth, UK: Rowman & Littlefield Publishers, 2008), 106–116, quoted in Covenant Eyes, *Pornography Statistics*, https://www.covenanteyes.com/pornstats/.

The long-term effect on porn actors and porn consumers can lead to sexual dysfunction and emotional dysfunction in future relationships and marriages. In a world designed to create pleasure, there's much pain happening behind the scenes. There's pain and, often, abuse in the background of the performance, and there will be future pain in the relationships of all who drink from the poisoned well of pornography.[7]

> **In a world designed to create pleasure, there's much pain happening behind the scenes.**

3. Porn has the same impact on your brain as an addictive drug.

The porn industry makes more money than all the major TV networks combined. It makes more money than all of professional sports combined. It is a global financial juggernaut, and because a lot of money is at stake, people don't want to admit that porn is destructive or addictive, but it is! Porn use is linked to depression, anxiety, sexism, sex crimes, divorce, and countless other physical, emotional, and relationship issues. The website fightthenewdrug.org contains compelling scientific evidence showing that ongoing exposure to porn has the same negative effect on the mind as a heroin addiction.[8]

---

7 Josh McDowell Ministry, *The Porn Phenomenon: The Impact of Pornography in the Digital Age* (Ventura, CA: Barna Group, 2016), p. ?.

8 *Hearing on the Brain Science Behind Pornography Addiction and the Effects of Addiction on Families and Communities: Hearing to US Senate Committee on Commerce, Science & Transportation*, November 18, 2004, (Judith Reisman, Jeffrey Sanitover, Mary Anne Layden, and James B. Weaver), http://www.ccv.org/wp-content/uploads/2010/04/Judith_Reisman_Senate_Testimony-2004.11.18.pdf.

4. Porn is the enemy of love.

We wholeheartedly believe this is true on a number of levels. As Christians, we can give you plenty of Bible verses—including Jesus saying that to look at a woman lustfully is to commit adultery in your heart and countless other passages about love, sex, and marriage—but even if you don't share our faith, the stats alone should be enough to make you want to stay away from porn for the rest of your life. It ruins marriages. It sabotages love. It is a primary source of disrespect toward women and even women disrespecting themselves. It creates the illusion of connection, but it's a manufacturer of disparities and divisions between men and women. It rewires the brain in devastating ways. It leads to widespread relational dysfunction and can desensitize the users from being able to experience sexual and/or emotional intimacy in later relationships.[9]

5. Most people don't see porn as wrong.

A recent study revealed that 96% of teenagers and young adults were either accepting or neutral when it came to their opinion of pornography. Only 4% believed it was wrong or a sin. This moral indifference is fueling a massive consumption of porn. In 2016, on one website alone, consumers watched 4.6 billion hours of porn. That's the equivalent of 17,000 entire lifetimes, and it happened all in one year and all on one website.[10]

---

9 Steven Stack, Ira Wasserman, and Roger Kern, "Adult Social Bonds and Use of Internet Pornography," *Social Science Quarterly* 85 (March 2004), 75–88.

10 Mo Isom, *Sex, Jesus, and the Conversations the Church Forgot* (Grand Rapids, MI: Baker, 2018), p. 64., p. 22.

Recently, the interactive website onlyfans.com, known for its adult content, stated that it was going to stop allowing people to post sexually explicit photos and videos on its site. However, the site ultimately reversed this decision due to many of their 130 million subscribers as well as their online adult performers pitching a fit about the decision. Many of the performers, who often provide exclusive, customized, and sexually explicit photos and videos for subscribers, were upset because they are able to make a substantial amount of their income through the website.[11] This story further proves the widespread acceptance of pornography in our culture today.

6. Porn and other cybersex-related activities can be as damaging to a marriage as an actual, physical affair.

In an in-depth project by researcher Jennifer P. Schneider, survey data measured the long-term impact of porn and other cybersex activities, which includes sexting and sharing sexually explicit images online. The research indicated that this activity is incredibly damaging to relationships, and those who are married indicated that the aftermath of these online activities can be every bit as painful as an actual physical affair. This is particularly harmful since most people don't see these

---

11 Shannon Bond, "OnlyFans Switches Its Stance on Sexually Explicit Content," NPR.org, August 25, 2021, https://www.npr.org/2021/08/25/1031067133/onlyfans-switches-its-stance-on-sexually-explicit-content#:~:text=OnlyFans%20Switches%20Its%20Stance%20On%20Sexually%20Explicit%20Content%20%3A%2-0NPR&text=OnlyFans%20Switches%20Its%20Stance%20On%20Sexually%20Explicit%20Content%20The%20subscription,a%20ban%20on%20such%20material..

online activities as a form of infidelity or even consider them as wrong.[12] Separate research has also found that the divorce rate for couples who view pornography is nearly twice as high as the divorce rate for couples who don't view porn.[13]

We can sum up many of the dehumanizing dangers of porn in a poignant quote from Pope John Paul II, who said, "There is no dignity when the human dimension is eliminated from the person. In short, the problem with pornography is not that it shows too much of the person, but that it shows far too little."

The Sexting Dilemma

She sat in our office crying. At first, I thought the tears were only because she missed her husband, who had been deployed to Afghanistan three months earlier, but as she began to open up to us, we quickly discovered that there was much more to her pain than just the physical distance between her and her husband. She was about to tell us a secret that she had sworn to herself that she would never tell anyone, but it was eating her up inside.

The young woman and her husband had started to drift apart in the months leading up to his deployment. Once the reality of the thousands of miles between them set in, she found herself desperately lonely. She had reconnected with an old "friend" via text, and he offered her support and

---

12 Jennifer P. Schneider, "Effects of Cybersex Addiction on the Family: Results of a Survey," *Sexual Addiction and Compulsivity: The Journal of Treatment and Practicum* 7, no. 1–2 (2000), 31–58.

13 Samuel L. Perry and Cyrus Schleifer, "Till Porn Do Us Part? A Longitudinal Examination of Pornography Use and Divorce," *The Journal of Sex Research* 55, no. 3 (2018), 284–96.

encouragement during those long, lonely nights. She felt safe confiding in him because he was in a different city. She knew the phone calls, text messages, and some occasional FaceTime calls would be the extent of the connection, so she deemed it harmless. That security caused her to let her guard down, and one night, one flirtatious text message with this "friend" led to another and another. Before she realized the reality of what was happening, she found herself engaging in an exchange of sexually explicit pictures and words with this friend.

Once the sexting exchange ended, she came back to her senses and realized the magnitude of what had happened. She texted her "friend" and explained that they had crossed lines that never should have been crossed and needed to break off all contact with one another. She blocked him from her phone and social media accounts and tried to put the whole incident behind her as if it had never happened. The problem was the secret kept eating away at her, and she knew that she had to get it out. She had painfully discovered the principle that we don't own our secrets; our secrets own us.

She made this tearful confession to us and asked what she should do next. She didn't want to tell her husband because she was sure this confession would cause irreversible damage to the intimacy and trust in their already tattered marriage. We prayed with her and encouraged her to remember that God's grace is bigger than our biggest mistake,

> **God's grace is bigger than our biggest mistake, and His forgiveness is instant and comes with no expiration date.**

and His forgiveness is instant and comes with no expiration date. We also shared the difficult truth that the Bible also clearly teaches that we need to confess our sins first to God and secondly to the one we sinned against, and in this case, she had sinned against her husband. We told her that ultimately, the choice was hers, but if a marriage is going to thrive, there can't be any secrets. In a marriage, secrets are as dangerous as lies, and until they are made known, they'll create an invisible barrier blocking your growth as a couple. A painful truth is always better than a hidden lie.

She waited until her husband returned from Afghanistan, so she could talk to him about it face-to-face. She told him everything, and he could see the remorse on her tearful face. He was hurt, understandably, but her courage inspired him to share some secrets of his own. After clearing the air and seeking forgiveness, they were both able to eventually move forward to a new level of health and strength in their relationship.

Sexting someone who is not your spouse is both a form of pornography and infidelity, and it should be avoided at all costs. Sexting with your spouse, however, is fine as long as you both feel comfortable and safe with it and are also very careful to keep these images and videos private. There are certainly risks involved with these images getting released, so be sure to do your research and, most importantly, make

> **With any sexual act, it's always good practice to pray about it and ask each other how this could potentially help or hurt your marriage and your walk with the Lord.**

sure you and your spouse are on the same page with whether or not sexting each other is okay.

With any sexual act, it's always good practice to pray about it and ask each other how this could potentially help or hurt your marriage and your walk with the Lord. If you *both* have peace about it, and you aren't including any other people—whether in person or virtually—in your sexual acts, then feel free to try new things with one another. We will talk about this in more detail later.

To the Husband Who Watches Porn: A Wife's Perspective

As we wrap up this chapter on porn, I (Ashley) want to share my perspective on how Dave's porn habit personally impacted me. We shared briefly about this earlier, but I want to unpack it in more detail here. I hope my testimony is a wake-up call for other men who are currently trapped in a cycle of porn use. I also hope it helps other wives going through the same situation know that they are not alone or to blame, and they can and will get through it. I know many women are consuming porn too, and many of the principles I'll share can also directly apply to your situation, but I want to specifically share some words for husbands so you can know how your porn use impacts your wife.

Early in our marriage, I logged into our computer and discovered that Dave had been looking at porn. I couldn't believe what I saw. My heart was beating out of my chest, and I seriously thought that somebody had broken into our home and surfed the web for porn. Not Dave. Not my Dave. We had a great marriage—at least, I thought we did.

All I could think was, *How could he do this to me? To us?... Am I not enough for him? Am I not pretty/skinny/sexy enough?... Doesn't he know this is wrong?... Didn't he know this would hurt me?*

I took an hour or so to process what I eventually realized and accepted as the truth: Dave had been looking at porn for a while. He had a porn addiction. My Dave. My husband. My hero.

I knew I had to address it. I called him at work and simply asked if he had something to tell me. He immediately confessed to the porn. It was like he'd been waiting for me to find out. He told me that he was glad it was out in the open now, and he knew it was wrong.

I would love to tell you that the days that followed were easy, but they weren't. I was so hurt. I felt ugly and unwanted. I could tell that Dave felt horrible about it. He wanted to stop doing this a long time ago, but he said he just couldn't stop through his own willpower.

As a Christian, he understood that he was lusting after the women in those images. He knew what Jesus stated so clearly in the Bible, that to lust at a woman is committing adultery in your heart. It goes directly against our marriage vows. Dave knew this, and yet, he struggled with it. Husbands, I share this with you, not to point fingers or make you feel bad. I share this because I want you to know what your porn habit does to your wife.

When a wife's husband watches porn, it breaks her heart.

It makes her feel like you cheated on her. It makes her doubt her beauty and sexual appeal. It causes her to have a deep insecurity about your marriage. It causes her anxiety and even depression. It makes her feel cheap, and she sees you as sleazy. It fractures the trust she has in you, and it immediately makes her lose respect for you. You may tell yourself the lies that so many other husbands in our culture believe. Lies like,

I'm not hurting anyone.

I'm not actually sleeping with another person, so it's not cheating.

What's wrong with me spicing up my sex life?

This is something I do alone, so it doesn't affect her.

Porn actually enhances my sex life because it gives me ideas of what we can do in the bedroom.

I'm a grown man, and I can do whatever I want to do. It's none of her business.

It's okay if I look at porn to meet my needs because she doesn't want to have sex as frequently as I do.

All of these are excuses that mask a huge problem and keep husbands intertwined in a terrible habit that can become a full-blown addiction. Husbands, if you are looking at porn, please get help and *stop* immediately. Go confess this to your wife. Don't hide it anymore. Seek God's forgiveness and your wife's forgiveness.

Then, take the steps necessary to regain her trust. Put accountability in place. Remove computers or other devices from hidden places. Get blockage software that will alarm a trusted friend or your wife any time you look up porn on your computer, like we shared earlier. Get rid of any television channels that show porn at night. Be willing to do whatever it takes to beat this and save your marriage. You can do this if you are willing to put in the work.

You must show your wife that you only have eyes for her. Show her that you want her and love her with all your heart. Give her your time and attention daily.

Those porn stars can't love you back. Don't trade the love of your life for a temporary, empty fix. Go to your wife and talk about your sexual desires and needs. Listen when she shares hers as well. Work together on having a God-honoring and sexually satisfying marriage. Don't settle for a counterfeit image to fulfill a need that only your wife should meet.

Porn is never the answer. It doesn't spice things up. It chokes out real intimacy between a husband and wife. Please know that if your husband watches porn (or if you as a woman are watching porn), there is hope. Dave and I grew stronger through this struggle, and you can too.

Don't let this toxic, counterfeit form of intimacy sabotage the real thing. Don't let it drive you into an addictive cycle of seeing self-gratification as a substitute for sexual intimacy with your spouse. On the flip side, don't let the hurt that a porn addiction has caused keep you from being willing to trust and be intimate with your spouse gain. Healing is a process, but taking steps in the direction of openness, consistency, and forgiveness are key. Porn is the enemy of love. Its promises are empty. It's a form of temporary pleasure that

> **Don't let the hurt that a porn addiction has caused keep you from being willing to trust and be intimate with your spouse gain.**

can create permanent scars, but God can heal you and give you freedom from the grip of porn just as He can free you from the habit of masturbation, which we will unpack next.

Questions to Consider:

1. Are you looking at porn together or separately?

2. If so, what is your motivation? Meeting your own sexual desires? Exploring what you like or dislike? Getting ideas of what to do in the bedroom? As a means of foreplay before intercourse?

3. Think about your own personal and/or collective reason for watching porn, and talk about it honestly, being mindful to listen without judgment.

4. How is watching porn cheapening your sex life? Is it like a drug for you? Is it a constant reel in your mind that crowds out your desire for your spouse? Talk about what porn has been taking from you.

5. If you have been watching porn, now is the time to confess this to your spouse, to repent before the Lord, and to seek God's forgiveness and your spouse's

forgiveness. Answer any and all questions your spouse might have and assure them that you love them and will do whatever it takes to regain their trust.

6. What are you both going to do to get porn out of your life? Download and use filtering software or apps on all devices? Removing your devices from hidden places? Getting off social media for a time? Getting rid of subscriptions or channels that have fueled your porn habit or addiction? Sharing the same passwords to make sure there is total accountability? Setting up an appointment with a Christian counselor to detox your mind and support your recovery process?

7. Make a plan together and stick to it. Have frequent check-ins and keep praying with and for one another. You will get through this and enjoy a marriage and life free from the bondage of porn!

CHAPTER 5

THE MASTURBATION MYTH

The prevalence of porn, along with many other counterfeit messages about sex and love in our culture, has created an epidemic of masturbation. As a quick disclaimer here at the start of this very touchy chapter, we want to remind you that you have an enormous amount of freedom in the bedroom as a married couple. Stimulating yourself and/or your spouse during sex is part of the fun and freedom of the marriage bed, and you should have no shame in it.

We're also not saying that it's necessarily wrong to masturbate alone while fantasizing about your spouse. Especially when separated by work or military deployment, we've heard from many couples who have worked to maintain their sexual connection through phone sex and other methods using masturbation. We're not here to referee anyone's marriage in this area, but we do want to highlight some concerning trends which are doing great damage to individuals and to marriages.

By all accounts, masturbation is at an all-time high. This is fueled in part by the prevalence of porn. It's also fueled by technologies aimed at making all forms of masturbation more pleasurable and accessible. The high-tech world of app-controlled vibrators and other devices has been promoted as a step toward female empowerment over their sexuality, but the trend has damaging effects. Many women are reporting symptoms of Dead Vagina Syndrome, where they've overstimulated their genitals to the point of numbness, and regular intercourse with a man can no longer stimulate them to the point of orgasm.

> We want to remind you that you have an enormous amount of freedom in the bedroom as a married couple.

Many men are also unable to perform sexually because of rampant masturbation and the specific lust and fetish-fueled fantasies that often accompany masturbation. We receive messages from both men and women whose individual lives and marriages have been negatively impacted by this trend. They believed the myth that masturbation was just harmless fun or "maintenance" if they weren't having sex as often as they wanted, but, before long, it created real issues.

When two people who are addicted to masturbation have sex with each other, it's nearly impossible for them to experience any real intimacy. Their minds have become so accustomed to racing to an orgasm fueled by whatever fantasy will get them there that they're rarely thinking about the person to whom they're making love. Their partner or spouse becomes only a warm body to enhance the orgasm.

When our minds are somewhere else during sex, then sex is still a form of masturbation instead of lovemaking. In this form of counterfeit climax, sex becomes nothing more than masturbating with a live penis instead of a plastic vibrator or masturbating inside of someone instead of in your own hand.

By rewiring our minds with false fantasies, masturbation can sabotage your sex life by making every climax a counterfeit climax. Even if we never physically have sex with another person, this lack of mental monogamy is an act of infidelity that can sabotage your sex life, and eventually, your marriage.

As for me (Dave) and my own story... actually, let me make a quick personal announcement. My mom reads everything Ashley and I write because she's a loving, supportive, encouraging, wonderful mom. Mom, I know you're reading this right now, but please skip the rest of this chapter. It's already awkward to admit what I'm about to admit, and it will be much more awkward knowing you're reading it! I love you. Now, please skip ahead. If you don't skip ahead, I might not ever be able to make eye contact with you again without blushing.

Okay, where was I? As for my own story, over the course of my teenage years, I masturbated literally thousands of times. I'd estimate I averaged one or two times per day for a solid decade. It was as much a part of my life as eating food, and, much like food, I felt I was going to die from starvation if I went too long without doing

> **By rewiring our minds with false fantasies, masturbation can sabotage your sex life by making every climax a counterfeit climax.**

it. That was awkward to admit, and just to give you fair warning, this conversation is probably going to get even more awkward. Stay with me as I share some intimate details from my past. This has an important point.

The early triggers to masturbate could be anything from seeing a lingerie ad on TV to seeing a girl in tight shorts walk by. I didn't have access to porn in those early adolescent years, but I did have a postcard hidden in my underwear drawer. I'd bought the postcard at a souvenir shop on a family trip to Myrtle Beach, and it had a titillating picture of a woman wearing a wet tee shirt which left little to the imagination. That fifty-cent postcard was like a gateway drug, eventually leading me to more graphic forms of pornography.

My masturbation habit was fed by porn, and the more I consumed porn, the more of a voracious appetite I had for masturbation. The more often I masturbated, the higher my sex drive became and the more porn I wanted to consume, so one sin fed the other in a vicious cycle, which felt inescapable at the time. The twin sins of porn and masturbation are so intricately connected, but of the two, masturbation was the more difficult to quit. Even after I finally broke free from pornography, it took me several more years to completely stop masturbating.

The irony of this cycle of pleasure-seeking sin is that I found so little pleasure in it. Whenever we give ourselves over to any sin, there's a numbness that begins to settle into our souls as a spiritual form of gangrene eats away at our inner selves. I was chasing pleasure, but I found little. I was a self-loathing fool, searching for fleeting moments of bliss instead of the steadfast presence of true joy and peace.

> **The irony of this cycle of pleasure-seeking sin is that I found so little pleasure in it.**

Like Esau in the Old Testament, I was trading my God-given blessings to sinfully satisfy a momentary hunger. With each of my returns to this sin, I found less pleasure and more misery. Despite the diminishing return of my actions, I proceeded with the desperation of an addict and the hopelessness of a fool. Once I finally came to my senses and committed to embracing God's grace and following God's plan, it was still a long journey until I found complete healing and deliverance.

Once I finally broke free from pornography, I realized that my brain had been rewired to play highlight reels of porn on a loop in my head. My thoughts were perpetually haunted by the remnants of porn. During the difficult period of mental detox, masturbation became like a form of methadone, which is what helps drug addicts wean off a drug while their bodies are going through detox. Even though I wasn't watching porn, I was still infected. My mind and body had become interconnected in an intricate web of sin resulting from years of lust.

Even all these years later, I still get flashbacks of my old, toxic thought life when certain images sneak into my brain through billboards or TV ads or unexpected steamy scenes on TV. It's a lifelong struggle, and staying away from porn and masturbation is like a form of sobriety. I've never been addicted to a substance, but in retrospect, I now recognize I was fully addicted and enslaved to these sins. Staying free from them still requires constant vigilance and intentionality.

If you're a woman reading this, you might be shocked or even assume my experience was abnormal. While some women have had experiences that mirror my own in these areas, this tends to disproportionally affect men. Most men reading this are probably nodding their heads in agreement because their experiences were likely similar to mine. Back in my school days, my buddies and I would talk openly about masturbation, and we even once had an informal contest to see who could masturbate the most in a month. I lost, but, assuming he was telling the truth, the guy who won almost doubled my total.

As a very important point of clarification, just because masturbation is "normal" in that almost all young men do it, that doesn't make it right. Even while I was caught up in the endless cycle of lust and self-gratification through masturbation, I knew it was wrong. I knew Jesus had taught about lust being a form of adultery, and I knew what the Bible had to say about not even having a hint of sexual immorality. Still, I found it easy to justify my so-called "minor sin" in light of the alternatives. I'd think justifying thoughts like,

> *Well, I'm not having sex with anybody, so nobody is getting hurt.*
>
> *It's my body, and I'm just doing routine maintenance. There are a lot worse things I could be doing. This is probably even healthy.*
>
> *One day, I'll have a wife, and I won't need to do this, and in the meantime, this is just something that has to be done.*

Of course, all my justifications were shallow lies meant to help me feel better about my sin. I thought I was in control, but I wasn't. I thought I could keep the sins of masturbation and lust locked neatly in a compartment of my mind and my life that would never really impact my relationships. I was wrong. Much like Jake in the second chapter, my justification of masturbation eventually led to other compromises, which caused even greater baggage and regrets.

Women and Vibrators

Recently, I (Ashley) was watching one of my favorite morning shows, and one of the top stories of the day centered around Gwyneth Paltrow and her widely popular skincare company, Goop®. During the interview, they talked about popular products in Paltrow's product line, including one "normally found at the back of an adult bookstore," referring to the line's popular vibrator for women. The host smiled uncomfortably and said, "Gwyneth, you do have some *products* that keep selling out… are you surprised?" Gwyneth smirked back, giggled, and said, "In a way, I'm not surprised. Look, I think that our sexuality is such an important part of who we are. […] If you think about it, we're on morning television, so we can't talk about female pleasure. […] One of the things we really believe in at Goop® is kind of eliminating shame from these topics."[14] With this story breaking on the morning news, the conversation pretty much ended on that note, but the message was clear. Vibrators have been around a long time, but they are more popular than ever at the moment. You can walk through a grocery aisle and see

---

14 Gwyneth Paltrow, interview by Savannah Guthrie, *Today*, April 15, 2021, https://www.today.com/parents/gwyneth-paltrow-blythe-danner-s-reaction-goop-products-t215132.

multiple magazines featuring articles about using vibrators. Many of the most popular television shows and movies paint the picture that if young women aren't using a vibrator regularly, then they are backward, out of touch with their bodies, and frankly, missing out. So, what are we to make of all of this?

Here's the thing: we do need to normalize women being able to understand and even talk about their bodies and sex without shame. However, this agenda to urge women to use vibrators and masturbate regularly to be "empowered" and even "healthy" is leading to negative consequences. Truth is, vibrators do not mimic a normal penis. They are often longer and girthier than the average man; not to mention, they can vibrate constantly and at different levels of intensity. Therefore, when a young woman has become accustomed to meeting her own sexual needs by frequently using a vibrator, she often can't experience the same orgasm while having penetrative intercourse with her husband. In fact, we often receive messages from women and men describing this dilemma. The wife often feels frustrated that she doesn't find sex with her husband to be as satisfying, and the husband feels inadequate that he can't bring his wife to orgasm as quickly or as intensely, if at all. It can cause a lot of marital issues, and most couples don't want to have to depend on a vibrator for the wife to experience an orgasm.

When it comes to sex, our bodies crave what brings the most pleasure, and we get used to our sexual routine. In other words, the more you do it, the more you crave it. Vibrators aren't wrong in and of themselves. In fact, most sex toys are permissible if you both feel safe and at peace using them to spice things up. Vibrators might be something you might want to use on occasion in the bedroom, but it shouldn't become something to depend on. Most importantly, women don't need to feel like they are weird or missing out if they don't masturbate and use vibrators regularly. Wives, don't be afraid to take time to understand what stimulates you; just don't do this on your own. As a married woman, ask your husband to touch different parts of you and try different positions. You would be surprised how different positions can create more intense orgasms. Try making love with you on top, along with nipple stimulation from your husband. Try it on a chair to achieve deeper penetration. Try giving and receiving oral sex with your husband. We don't share these ideas to put any pressure on you or to make you feel uncomfortable. It is imperative that you both feel comfortable with any of these things. We just want you to know that God gives you and your spouse a lot of room to explore and enjoy one another's bodies. Sex should be fun and pleasurable for you both, but most of all, it is about connection.

> **Sex should be fun and pleasurable for you both, but most of all, it is about connection.**

Sex Robots and the Future of Tech-Based Lust

As both porn and masturbation-based technology continue to grow in prominence and profitability, the next phase in the evolution of its counterfeit message is in creating more high-tech ways for people to experience sexual fulfillment without another human being involved either in person or on screen. We live in an era where technology is advancing at a dizzying speed. Many of the innovators at the forefront of these technological advancements are sadly those who are peddling pornography and other tech-based forms of sexual entertainment. The latest craze in the tech-sex boom follows the growing demand for sex robots.

A recent local news story reported that Texas is set to open its first "brothel" made up of high-tech sex robots. We watched in amazement as the anchors seamlessly transitioned from local weather and sports to featuring creepily lifelike robots equipped with artificial intelligence and designed to respond to the sexual commands and preferences of their male customers. The news story became a sort of advertisement for the brothel by giving the hourly rates for rental and the sale prices for those customers who wanted their own on-demand robotic sex slave in the comfort of their own home.[15]

The story featured interviews with concerned residents who thought the whole concept was seedy and creepy, but those profiting from the new boom in sex robots argued that it's simply meeting a service. It's simply supply and demand. Beyond the pure capitalism of it, there are no actual victims. It's essentially a high-tech form of masturbation. Many argued that the on-demand option for sexual gratification will lower the demand for sex trafficking and instances of sexual assault.

---

15 Deborah Wrigley, "Toronto Businessman Brings Sex Robot Brothel to the Galleria Area," ABC 13 News, September 21, 2018, https://abc13.com/technology/toronto-businessman-brings-sex-robot-brothel-to-the-galleria-area-/4306146/.

These arguments are clearly wrong and perpetuated only by those with selfish motives.

As we pondered the future of how technology will facilitate sexual sin for profit, we had several initial thoughts. First, we noticed that all these sex robots were designed to look like young women barely eighteen years of age. Some of them appeared to look like girls even younger than the legal age of consent. Troubling. Our minds also flashed back to all the Old Testament warnings against bestiality, which is essentially using any nonhuman body for sexual gratification. God's Word has always given clear warnings about the misuse of sex in any form.

For all the Old Testament parallels and the creepy grossness of the entire concept, what troubles us the most has to do with the disrespect toward women that this practice will undoubtedly ignite. You might argue that it's impossible to show disrespect to women by how you treat a robot. I'd argue that it matters how you treat the image of a person and that it significantly impacts how you treat people in general. In fact, I'd argue that it matters a lot.

The human mind is a training ground for our beliefs, and our beliefs become our actions. If a child practices loving and nurturing a baby doll, the child will, most likely, love and nurture a real-life baby sibling in a similar way. If an adult uses and objectifies a doll made in the image of a woman, his mind will eventually justify the

> **The human mind is a training ground for our beliefs, and our beliefs become our actions.**

objectification of actual women. His mind will be rewired to see sex as a selfish act where it's impossible to actually abuse a sexual partner because, like his robots, she exists only for his own sexual pleasure. Her pleasure (or even her consent) aren't consequential matters as long as he gets what he wants.

If you regularly have sex with an object that you own, it won't be long before you treat a human sexual partner like an object that you own. Even a spouse can start to be seen as nothing more than an object that exists for your on-demand pleasure. That's the lie fueled by masturbation. We start to believe that others exist for our own sexual gratification.

These counterfeit human bodies designed to stimulate orgasm are literally the embodiment of a counterfeit climax. When we become willing to trade real intimacy for a completely self-focused, self-indulgent replacement, we're planting poisonous seeds in our own minds and hearts. These sex robots are a high-tech form of porn, and porn in all its forms ultimately harms all who consume it. It might seem easy to justify viewing porn as a harmless form of sexual exploration but watching porn as a means of meeting your sexual needs is like drinking poison as a means of quenching your thirst. It might seem to satisfy you at that moment, but it will always hurt you in the end.

The Power to Do Difficult Things

If you currently feel caught up in a cycle of lust and masturbation, maybe you feel powerless to break free. We want to end this chapter by giving you some encouragement. You *can* break free.

You can do difficult things. You're stronger than you think, and you can do anything you set your mind to with God's help.

We recently purchased an online video conference for our older sons. We ended up learning just as much as our kids did from the lessons taught in this video. The conference is called "Do Hard Things," and it is taught by twin brothers Alex and Brett Harris, who were still teenagers themselves at the time the video was recorded. These high-achieving brothers also wrote a bestselling book of the same title.[16]

Our sons Cooper and Connor moaned and complained when we fired up the laptop and started the videos. They would have much rather been playing video games, but we told them that these videos are worthwhile. Within a few minutes of the teaching, my boys had stopped fidgeting and complaining and were captivated by what they were learning.

Of all the stories and principles shared in the videos, one stood out to them both. The twins explained how elephants are tamed and trained for work in India. A full-grown elephant has the power to knock over a tree with his brute strength, but the elephant will not resist when tied up with a simple rope. The animal will give up at the first sign of resistance.

The reason why the elephant won't break free from a rope is because when the elephant was a baby, the trainer would bind his leg with thick chains and uncomfortable shackles. The baby elephant would fight and strain until the shackles cut into his ankles and caused great pain. Eventually, he would stop

---

16 Alex Harris and Brett Harris, "Do Hard Things Conference" DVDs, *The Rebelution*, https://www.dohardthings.com/conference.

fighting against the chain. As time passed and the elephant gave up the fight, the chain would be replaced with a light rope, but he still never fought back.

Even as the elephant grew into adulthood and had the strength to lift heavy logs with his trunk or drag tons of weight with his enormous strength, he still felt powerless against the rope. In his simple mind, he believed he must give up at the first sign of resistance because, in the past, he had failed to break free. The elephant had no concept of the strength he possessed, and so he could be easily controlled by something far weaker than himself. He remained in lifelong bondage simply because he didn't know his own strength.

As it relates to the topic of lust and masturbation, maybe you have given up and resigned yourself to the myth that you are powerless over this situation. I (Dave) was in that same place. I was allowing the "rope" of masturbation to keep me bound in a slave-like cycle of lust and self-gratification. I had failed in the past to break free through my own willpower, so, in shame and defeat, I believed that I would always be in bondage.

Maybe you feel powerless to break free from the bondage of lust and masturbation, but you are stronger than you think. Not only can you do difficult things, you have a power at your disposal that is even greater than the mighty strength of the elephant.

We have more strength than we realize, but our strength alone will never be enough. Thankfully, our strength alone never has to be enough. Jesus Himself wants to fight this battle with us and for us. He's waiting for the invitation.

Praying for strength in areas like masturbation might

seem awkward, but no conversation with God should ever feel awkward. Our heavenly Father already sees our struggles and shortcomings. He's never shocked or surprised by our sins. He wants to bring forgiveness and the opportunity for a fresh start.

Whatever we feed gets bigger. When we overfeed our bodies, our bodies grow bigger. When we feed our bank account with financial deposits, our balance grows bigger. When we feed our lustful thoughts with a steady diet of lust and self-gratification, our desires will grow bigger and eventually give birth to unhealthy expressions of desire.

Challenge yourself to carefully consider what you're feeding. Are you feeding your mind and soul with the truth of God's Word? The more Scripture we put into our minds, the more we'll be safeguarding our eyes and hearts from wandering off track. The Bible says, "I have hidden your word in my heart, that I might not sin against you" (Psalm 119:11).

If we're not feeding our minds a steady diet of God's Word, we won't have any appetite for it. If we're feeding our minds a diet of lustful thoughts playing on-demand, our appetites will be driven by lust. You don't have to be bound by the rope of lust, shame, or regret when God has already given you the strength to break free.

> **If we're not feeding our minds a steady diet of God's Word, we won't have any appetite for it. If we're feeding our minds a diet of lustful thoughts playing on-demand, our appetites will be driven by lust.**

Some of the heaviest and most damaging baggage is the

result of past abuse. In the next chapter, we'll address this heavy topic and offer hope to those of have been impacted by it.

Questions to Consider:

1. Is personal masturbation something you do regularly?

2. If so, how has this affected your view of sex?

3. How has this affected your relationship with your spouse?

4. How has this affected your sex life? What has it taken away from you both? Less desire for sex? Less frequency? Sex that feels less satisfying or like just going through the motions?

5. Talk about these answers with your spouse. If you have been fulfilling your sexual desires through frequent masturbation, confess this to your spouse, repent to the Lord, and seek God's and your spouse's forgiveness.

6. What could you do to combat the desire to masturbate? Pray about it and make a plan together.

CHAPTER 6

OVERCOMING THE SCARS OF THE PAST

Some of the most deeply embedded counterfeit thoughts about love and sex are the ones inflicted through past trauma, regret, or abuse. In our work, we've seen firsthand that the trauma of past abuse (physical, emotional, and sexual) can be devastating. Many of those who have been victimized in the past have also carried an untrue stigma that they can't speak out or that the abuse was somehow their own fault.

For those of you who have suffered from abuse, we want to help you find strength by knowing you're not alone. Hope and help are available. Every one of us has, in some way, been affected by trauma and/or abuse. One of the most egregious forms of trauma is abuse. Sadly, abuse can even happen in places where we should feel completely safe, even places like the church.

A decade ago, I (Dave) was working at a church in Florida. It was a vibrant, growing church, but one of the youth pastors was hiding a sinister secret. This pastor was, on the surface, a pillar of the community. His social media posts and public persona painted the picture of a rock-solid family

> Every one of us has, in some way, been affected by trauma and/or abuse.

man who adored his wife and kids and faithfully lived out the message he preached to his youth group. But his carefully crafted reputation came crashing down the day he was arrested for having a yearlong sexual affair with a fifteen-year-old girl in his youth group.

I remember watching the news story of his arrest. He had been such a revered and dignified leader, but his mug shot depicted a distraught and humiliated hypocrite. He had broken the hearts of his wife and children. He had caused immeasurable damage to the church he had professed to love. He had shattered the innocence of a young girl and wounded her with lifelong emotional scars. Our community was left wondering how a man who had appeared to be so trustworthy, faithful, and respectable could be capable of such heinous acts.

He later confessed that he had harbored fantasies about this girl and others in the youth group but had wrongly assumed that his fantasies were harmless. He never believed he would act on them. He was disciplined in other areas of his life, so he had a prideful and misguided view of his own personal strength and restraint. He believed he was a good person and even a good pastor. In his mind, his fantasies were just a natural way to blow off steam and add some excitement to his predictable routine of work, bills, kids, and life in suburbia.

He had compartmentalized parts of his mind where his dark fantasies could live, but sinful fantasies never stay in the tidy compartments we try to keep them in. As he would later confess, the first time he had sexual contact with this girl, it happened so effortlessly because he had replayed this scenario in his mind a thousand times. He had systematically desensitized himself and removed the moral compass that had guided him all his life.

I'm sure he never imagined he would be committing statutory rape in the sound booth of a sanctuary after a youth service, but on an otherwise uneventful Wednesday night, that's exactly what happened. Whatever thoughts we allow to replay in our minds will eventually shape our actions. In an instant, his "harmless" fantasies had given birth to unimaginable consequences for himself, for his victim, and for countless others.

Tragically, I've spoken to many women over the years who have been similarly abused by men in positions of authority. I've also spoken to men who experienced sexual abuse. I've heard heartbreaking tales of harassment, exploitation, and assault at the hands of people once trusted and admired. This list of abusers and womanizers includes preachers, bosses, educators, relatives, politicians, mentors, and a myriad of other categories. These people have misused their influence, selfishly defiling and disregarding others as if they were nothing more than disposable objects or a game of sexual conquest.

One of the most common trends among these predators is the ability to keep up a respectable public persona while living a secret life of sexual deviance. In their arrogance, they seem to believe that their actions are consequence-free, but there is always a high cost for living a double life. We can't compartmentalize our lives and believe that what we do in secret won't eventually come out. Another way to say "compartmentalize" is "compartmental lies." Those lies will catch up with us. They always do.

Scripture gives us the sobering warning that everything done in secret will eventually be shouted from rooftops, and what is done in the darkness will always be illuminated eventually. All along the way, the damage done by our choices

> **We can't compartmentalize our lives and believe that what we do in secret won't eventually come out.**

will continue to build. The consequences for sexual sin create repercussions not only for those directly involved but also for many others who become collateral damage in the aftermath. Temporary pleasure is never worth the permanent regrets.

Perhaps the greatest tragedy in this entire situation with my former colleague is that all the pain and devastation were completely preventable. It never had to happen. It never should have happened. I'm sure he would give anything to travel back in time and undo the damage his reckless actions caused, the ripple effect that spread through an entire community. As he sits alone in a prison cell, I'm sure he's haunted by the pain his family and young victim feel.

This chapter isn't just meant to give comfort to those who have been abused; it also serves as a warning for us all not to fall into the trap of becoming abusers. Most abusers don't set out to abuse others; they simply remove accountability from their lives and make one little compromise at a time until they find themselves doing despicable things they never dreamed they'd do.

We need accountability. If you have started down a dark road, stop! Get help. Get accountability. Turn yourself into the police if you've already crossed legal boundaries. Have the courage to get help and to face the consequence for what you may have already done.

Maybe you were abused, and you're acting out what happened to you. You are not responsible for what happened to you when you were victimized, but you are completely responsible for the decisions you're making now. Don't create more victims! Get help. Break the terrible cycle.

It Can Happen to Anyone, Anywhere

Most of the stories we hear in the media are about older men victimizing young women, but this isn't the only abusive dynamic. Many men and boys have also been the victims of abuse, and sometimes the shame carried by male victims of abuse can manifest later in life in a myriad of ways. The male victims of domestic violence are much less likely to report their injuries because they carry a feeling of shame, thinking they should have been strong enough to stop it. The point here is that whether you're male or female, a young child, or a full-grown adult when you experience abuse, the abuse was and is *not* your fault.

Some forms of abuse are blatant, like an adult physically or sexually assaulting a child. Other forms of abuse are more subtle. When there is gaslighting, verbal abuse, or emotional abuse, the victim might wrestle with reality and wonder if they've really been abused at all. Those mind games are a form of abuse in and of themselves.

Some forms of abuse are de-personalized in that it's not directed toward one specific person, but we are collectively impacted by unwanted exposure to sexual things. Social media and the prevalence of smartphones in every pocket have opened the world up to this kind of abuse. We don't often think of these kinds of activities as "abuse," but we've seen firsthand in our own home that these counterfeit messages about sex can have very negative impacts.

> Some forms of abuse are de-personalized in that it's not directed toward one specific person, but we are collectively impacted by unwanted exposure to sexual things.

A few years ago, our oldest son came home from his first day of eighth grade with a look of bewilderment on his face. We immediately started peppering him with questions about his first day, and he mumbled a few short answers as he checked his phone. Like most adolescent boys, he seemed much more interested in getting to his video games than he was in carrying on a conversation about school.

We bribed him with some snacks to keep the conversation going, and before he finished the last bite of a pepperoni Hot Pocket, he asked us one question that nearly left us both speechless. He cleared his throat and shuffled his feet a bit as he searched for the words, and then he finally blurted out, "Do girls like it when boys send them pictures of their penises?"

As you can imagine, this question sparked some immediate follow-up questions from us. We tried not to act shocked because we've found that the calmer we stay, the more the boys will tell us. The moment we freak out, they shut down. We played it cool and kept asking questions, which finally revealed that some of the boys on the bus had been taking pictures of their genitalia, showing the pictures to the other kids on the bus, and texting those images to other kids.

One boy was flashing a picture and laughing, saying, "Girls love getting these pictures texted to them!" The boy tried to put his phone right in front of our son's face, but he pushed the phone away and made it clear that he had no interest in participating. Our son was shocked by this kind of behavior, but he was also perplexed by that brazen boy's statement.

He asked, *"Do girls really like it when guys do that? Is this actually how relationships are supposed to work?"* We told him that he had done the right thing by standing up to this kind of obscene behavior, and I (Ashley) reassured him that, "No, I can promise you that girls certainly do not like receiving pictures like this. They might giggle out of shock or nervousness, but inside they'll be disgusted, offended, and possibly even terrified. Boys should always treat girls with respect, and what these boys are doing is both disrespectful and illegal."

In the work that we do with couples and families, we've learned that "naked pics" are commonplace for many teens and adults today, and it's happening everywhere. Nearly every person has had encounters with seeing unwanted sexual images, and while these instances can seem relatively innocuous compared to the more graphic examples of abuse we shared early in the chapter, these encounters can still leave lasting negative remnants.

Past Trauma with Present Ramifications

I (Dave) am convinced that present pain can be rooted in painful events from the past. Childhood trauma can create deep scars and lasting effects. Sometimes this pain can manifest itself in peculiar ways.

When I was six years old, my cousin, Tina, and her dad died on the same day in a boating accident. Tina was part of my family, but she was also one of my closest friends. The death of her and my uncle completely rocked my young mind. More than a generation later, the ripple effect from that single tragedy continues to impact my family.

To further complicate my feelings of loss, I was also feeling guilt and shame because Tina and I had touched each other in sexual ways. We knew that "touching private parts" was wrong, but our childhood curiosity propelled us to forbidden exploration. These experiences created a massive amount of confusion and shame after her death. My first-grade brain had no capacity to process the trauma and emotion I was feeling.

My dad took me fishing a couple weeks after the funeral. We caught a fish, and then Dad fileted it with his knife. As I watched that fish being cut up, somehow, my mind connected the fish's death to my cousin's death on the water. At that moment, seafood became completely unappetizing. I was repulsed by the smell of it and the taste of it. Even microwaveable fish sticks had lost their luster.

All these decades later, I still don't eat seafood. I'd like to. I've tried to. Intellectually, I understand that my aversion to seafood is completely illogical, and I should be able to enjoy it. Still, something happened in my young mind's hardwiring that has never been completely undone. I'm still as repulsed by seafood as I was many years ago when the tragedy took place.

I hadn't talked about or thought about my childhood trauma in a long time until I recently started seeing a counselor. As I've been working through all sorts of issues (and I have plenty), the story of Tina came up in one of our sessions. Even though I hadn't thought about it in years, my eyes started forming tears the moment I began to retell the story. My youngest son is now the same age I was when Tina died, so my counselor suggested I visualize myself at that same age and think back to my childhood self with a lot of compassion and think about what I'd tell him now if I could.

Looking at my son's innocence and unbridled joy helps me imagine what I must have been like back then. Picturing my son going through the same tragedy and shame is heartbreaking. If he experienced what I did, I would just want to hold him and reassure him that everything is going to be okay. I'd want him to know that he's not alone and he doesn't have to be afraid.

If I could go back and have a few moments with my six-year-old self, I think I'd say something like, "Hey buddy, I know you're really sad, but it's going to get better. I know you feel really guilty for some of the things you and Tina did together, but Jesus forgives you, and you don't need to keep feeling ashamed. I know you think about death a lot, and you're afraid of it, but you don't have to be. You're going to live to be old, and when it's the right time, Jesus will take you to heaven, which is the most fun and least scary place you can imagine. Tina is having an amazing time in heaven right now, and you'll be there someday too. For now, Jesus wants you to live an amazing life here on earth and have a beautiful family of your own someday. You'll have some other sad stuff happen because that's just part of life, but you're going to have so many great things happen too. It's going to be a great adventure!"

Maybe you are still carrying some residual aftermath of earlier loss, tragedy, or regret. Everybody carries something, and the invisible weights we carry tend to be the heaviest of all. You might benefit from pulling up a chair and imagining your younger self sitting in it. Picture yourself at your point of greatest loss or greatest regret. Talk to yourself with compassion. Give yourself grace just like Jesus has already. Give thanks that God carried you through that difficult time and start releasing the baggage you're still carrying.

For me, the long-term aftermath of that early trauma is minor compared to what many people are carrying. I live with a dietary quirk that doesn't really alter the quality of my life in any significant way, but many people experience much

> **Everybody carries something, and the invisible weights we carry tend to be the heaviest of all.**

deeper scars. Perhaps a past trauma has left you with baggage that's much more noticeable than a dislike for seafood. Maybe you've lived with real physical pain, emotional pain, or relational brokenness of things that took place decades earlier (or possibly more recently). Maybe your current family dynamic is a constant reminder of wounds from the past. Whatever you've been through, with God's help, you can and will overcome it.

I've been impacted through the years by friends who have overcome unimaginable tragedies in their past through their faith and relentless hope. I've seen many friends who have allowed wounds from their past to shape their lives in ways much more significant than avoiding seafood. I've known people who numb their past pain by overdrinking or overindulging in food. I've known women who felt unloved as little girls who became promiscuous as young women as a cry for attention and affirmation from men. I've known men who felt powerless or unloved as boys who became obsessively driven and aggressive men who were willing to hurt others if it meant that they themselves never had to feel powerless again.

It seems to me that most of these past wounds with present manifestations stem from either feeling powerless or unloved. I felt powerless when my cousin and uncle died, but I always knew I was loved by God and my family, and that love gave me strength. When a child feels both powerless and unloved—often because of abuse and/or the absence of a father—that child might grow up trying in vain to numb the pain caused years ago, much like Madison's experience that we described in Chapter 3.

"Father wounds" are some of the deepest wounds. Thankfully, I had and still have a wonderful and loving father and mother. They gave my brothers and me such a safe environment in which to grow up and a solid foundation for our futures. I know that many were not so blessed.

I believe some of the greatest world-changers are the unsung men who grew up with an absent or abusive father, and yet they themselves choose to break the generational cycle and become present and loving fathers for their own children. This also applies to the courageous women who grew up in broken home environments, and yet they choose to change their family legacy by becoming loving mothers. They are the real heroes.

If you are living with pain from your past, I know those scars can still feel like fresh wounds. Whether your pain is rooted in past tragedy, loss, abandonment, failure, abuse, or anything else, the cause isn't nearly as important as the solution. The solution, in short, is Jesus.

Healing begins by allowing our Savior to comfort us and remembering that our identity is defined completely by Him. We're not defined by our past pains, our past failures, or even our past successes. We're defined by the fact that the God of the universe loves us and has adopted us into His eternal family as a result of His grace and our faith in Him. The more we stay connected to Him as a branch must stay connected to the vine, the more His healing can sustain us and heal us.

We'll experience this connection when we make our daily walk with Him a priority through prayer, reading the Bible, and pursuing hope and growth like you're doing now as you read this book. We also experience His healing through healthy relationships with other people and by using our God-given gifts and skills to serve others.

> **Healing begins by allowing our Savior to comfort us and remembering that our identity is defined completely by Him.**

God's plan for healing is always rooted in relationships (both relationships with Him and with others). Don't try to do it alone. I know you've been hurt deeply, but you've been loved even more deeply.

You Don't Have to Face It Alone

If you're carrying the invisible scars of past abuse, please get help. Talk to a trusted friend. If you're married, tell your spouse. Schedule an appointment with a Christian counselor who specializes in past trauma. You don't have to face this alone. God's plan for healing always happens within the context of relationships.

Even if you feel alone right now, know that God is with you. He is close to the brokenhearted (Psalm 34:18). He is walking with you in this pain, and He will never leave you or abandon you (Hebrews 13:5).

If you have never experienced abuse, be grateful, but also look for ways to be a support for your spouse if they have experienced this trauma. Be a safe place for your spouse to process their feelings. Be patient, tender, and supportive in every way you can. Encourage them to talk to a professional Christian counselor or attend a support group. Even when you don't have the words, let your spouse know by your presence and your support that you're going to walk every step of the journey with them.

> **If you have never experienced abuse, be grateful, but also look for ways to be a support for your spouse if they have experienced this trauma.**

Questions to Consider:

1. Have you ever experienced sexual trauma, regret, or any other form of abuse?

2. If so, think about it. What feelings come to the surface? Shame? Anger? Sadness? Confusion? Avoidance? Pray and ask the Lord to heal any brokenness in your heart and to know that you are deeply loved.

3. Have you ever told your spouse about what you went through? If not, tell your spouse what happened to you. If your spouse tells you about their sexual trauma, be sure to listen intently and offer support.

4. Have you ever talked to a Christian counselor about your past trauma? If not, we encourage you to find a counselor in your area. Many local churches have information about this and often offer support groups as well. Healing is possible!

CHAPTER 7

TRUST ISSUES

Many single people and couples struggle with the counterfeit message that complete trust is impossible. A lack of trust is what keeps some single people from ever pursuing marriage, and it keeps some married people from ever experiencing total and complete intimacy. They live in a pseudo-trust dynamic where there is an illusion of trust on the surface, but it isn't authentic. Usually, their damaged views of trust are rooted in some betrayal from the past. We've seen this dynamic have an ongoing effect in the marriages of quite a few of our close friends, including Josh and Cindy.

Our friends, Josh and Cindy, have been married for more than twenty years, and they have four beautiful children. They're involved in full-time ministry, and from the outside, their marriage and family don't have a problem in the world. We know that every couple has some

> **A lack of trust is what keeps some single people from ever pursuing marriage, and it keeps some married people from ever experiencing total and complete intimacy.**

issues, but we were still somewhat surprised when they reached out to us for help, feeling like their marriage had reached a point of crisis.

Josh is the one who called. He said that their marriage had always been good, but Cindy seemed to have trust issues. Other than a short-lived struggle with porn in the early years of their marriage, where he confessed to Cindy and worked to regain her trust, Josh had given her no other reasons to doubt his commitment and fidelity. Still, she seemed to always be testing him. For reasons he couldn't explain, Cindy never felt completely secure with his commitment to her.

She was in the habit of giving him lists of tasks to do and then grading him on how well and how quickly he completed the to-do items on her list. He felt like he was always being evaluated in some kind of warped game that he could never win. He desperately wanted to let Cindy know that she could trust him, but, for some reason, it seemed like complete trust and intimacy were always missing.

After some long conversations about their backstory, we finally understood why trust was so elusive for Cindy. It had little to do with Josh. It had everything to do with Cindy's dad. When she was a little girl, she had been a Daddy's Girl. Her dad could do no wrong in her eyes. He was her hero.

During a very impressionable time in her adolescent years, her dad abruptly left the family. He was having an affair with a much younger woman, and he chose a life with his mistress over his wife and kids. Cindy was abandoned by her hero, and as you can imagine, she was completely devastated. It rocked her world, and, even decades later, she was still reeling from the shock of it all. If she couldn't trust her father, her hero, then she felt like she couldn't trust anybody.

Without realizing it, she was constantly testing Josh. Her to-do lists were one of the many ways she was seeing if he could continue to meet her standard of trust. Although he was doing nothing to betray her, she was always waiting for the other shoe to drop. She never let herself become fully comfortable or secure in the marriage. She was convinced he was going to leave the same way her father had.

Her perpetual fear was a source of great frustration for Josh because he was essentially being punished for someone else's actions. This often happens in marriage. When we've been wounded by the betrayal of a parent or ex-partner or anyone else who had once had our trust, it makes it much more difficult to trust again. Still, these issues have to be addressed, or past betrayals will keep sabotaging our current peace.

The 5 Stages of Trust

"Trust is built in drops, but it's lost in buckets." —Jimmy Evans

To help Josh and Cindy, along with other couples, work through trust issues, we've developed a simple visual to help couples identify where they currently are in their trust levels. We believe there are five levels of trust. They operate in stages that build on one another until reaching the ultimate goal of trust, simply defined as "comfort." When we fully trust someone, we are able to comfortably be at peace in the relationship, and we're not afraid to be vulnerable and fully trusting. In marriage, if you aren't at that level of complete comfort with each other, you need to work together to identify the reasons why.

When trust is broken or fragile in your relationship, you need to start at the first level of trust and recommit to the relationship. Commitment is the first layer of trust. When trust has been broken, the first step in rebuilding it is always to remind yourself of your commitment to the relationship.

The next layer is communication. Complete honesty and ongoing communication are the keys to building intimacy. Communication does for a marriage what breathing does for the lungs. It's crucial for survival.

The next phase is consistency. This is the key ingredient in building or rebuilding trust. We build it a little at a time, but we can lose trust all at once through a betrayal and then have to start the entire process over again.

The next stage is courage. It requires courage to make yourself vulnerable. Choosing to trust someone isn't just a feeling; it's a choice. It's a conscious, courageous choice to be close enough to them that they have the ability to hurt you. That might sound scary, but that kind of vulnerability and nakedness is the only place real love and real intimacy can live.

> **Communication does for a marriage what breathing does for the lungs. It's crucial for survival.**

If we keep our guard up all our life, we might not get hurt, but we'll never experience real love either. We settle for survival instead of intimacy. We put walls around our hearts that can create hardness and bitterness instead of tenderness. Have the courage to let your walls down. It's the only way to experience true trust, love, and intimacy.

Once we do that, we'll settle into a place of comfort. This is the bullseye. This is the goal of every relationship. It's a place of vulnerability but also a place of safety when you're with someone who has earned your trust. Here's what this dynamic looks like:

Comfort is the goal. It's having such an intimate bond of trust that you can truly rest in the relationship, knowing that the other person loves you and will never intentionally harm you. We know that many reading this book have been at the comfort stage, but sadly, trust has been lost through your own actions or the actions of your spouse. Many write us and ask what to do once the trust has been shattered. Specifically, when the ultimate betrayal happens (an affair), couples wonder what to do to rebuild trust. They often wonder if it's even possible. Rebuilding trust from that kind of devastating betrayal can be a long and arduous process, but healing is possible.

Rebuilding Trust After an Affair

"I'm having an affair." If you've said these words, then you understand the weight they carry. They are daggers to the heart and can be deadly to a marriage, but there is still hope for healing and restoration. If you are the spouse who committed the affair, your words and actions in the days that lie ahead are essential and have the power to heal or break down your marriage even further.

As the one who had the affair, it is important to remember that your spouse will experience a wide range of emotions after hearing your confession, and it will most likely take them a long time to heal. So, please give them the time and space they need to process their emotions so you both can continue to move toward restoration.

You might be thinking, is that even possible? Can a marriage truly be saved after an affair? Yes, vows have been broken. Yes, trust must be earned once again. Yes, it's messy, emotional, and hard. However, after years of meeting with and talking to couples both in person and online, we can tell you that it *is* possible. However, it takes lots of work and constant prayer. So, if you had an affair, here are four crucial steps you must take to save your marriage:

1. Start with REPENTANCE and CONFESSION to God and your spouse.

The very first step that must take place when you have had an affair and realize that what you are doing is wrong is to stop seeing this other person immediately. Cut off all contact in person, online, or elsewhere. Change your daily patterns to make sure you won't run into them, change your phone number, and shut down your social media accounts for as long as it takes to make sure you won't be contacted or be tempted to reach the other person. Then, repent. Ask God to forgive you for being unfaithful and to help you refocus on your commitment to your spouse. Ask Him to give you strength to confess, and then do it. God will help you through this, but it won't be easy. It will be gut-wrenching, emotional, and heartbreaking. However, you must confess in order for healing to take place. The sooner you end the adulterous relationship, repent, and admit to the affair, the better. No matter how awful and ugly the truth may seem, once you bring it to light, that is when God begins to heal our hearts.

2. Be completely HONEST and OPEN with your spouse about EVERYTHING.

You don't necessarily need to tell your spouse all the details of an adulterous relationship, but you must be willing to answer any and all questions that your spouse may have. Trust has been broken. The process to regain trust is a slow one, and this can only happen with full transparency. With that said, I (Ashley) want to remind the innocent spouse to be cautious when asking for specifics. It is hard for us to get things out of our minds once they are in there. We don't want to keep replaying images of our spouse cheating on us with someone else over and over in our thoughts. This will only hinder the healing process. It's okay to want specific details to better understand what led to the affair, but knowing the details isn't going to change the fact that it happened.

> **The process to regain trust is a slow one, and this can only happen with full transparency.**

3. Fully COMMIT to saving your marriage even when it feels ugly and uncomfortable.

The only way a marriage can survive and even thrive after an affair is by both the husband and the wife recommitting to one another. However, as the spouse who committed the affair, this recommitment starts with you. You must take the first step by showing your spouse how committed you are to doing whatever it takes to regain their trust and save your marriage. This will encourage your spouse to give you and your marriage a chance to heal. Both of you must be willing to go through all the emotions that follow the news of an affair—and your emotions will be all over the place. The innocent spouse is allowed to be angry but must do their best to not sin in their anger by punishing the guilty spouse with hateful words and actions. As the spouse who was unfaithful, you must face the consequences of your sinful actions and approach your spouse with tenderness and humility.

Both of you must also be willing to do things differently, and this can be very frustrating and awkward at times. A marriage counselor or pastor is extremely helpful in navigating through all of these steps and helping a couple move forward. We cannot forget the past, but we can move forward with recommitted hearts, healthier habits, and a deeper understanding of God and one another with God's help through prayer and counsel.

4. Be patient with your spouse's willingness to FORGIVE and TRUST you.

> Even if that person wrongs you seven times a day and each time turns again and asks forgiveness, you must forgive. (Luke 17:4)

We don't believe anyone sets out on a quest to commit adultery and bust up their family. It happens one small bad decision at a time. One "meaningless" flirtation that leads to a lunch date at work. One silly text with an inside joke and a secret meeting. One inappropriately vulnerable conversation that leads to an intimate relationship. Any of us can fall prey to this temptation when boundaries are crossed, and we proceed without caution. Even so, when one spouse decides to have an affair, they choose to break their marriage vows. The other spouse is not to blame. However, no spouse is ever completely innocent of sin in marriage. We all fall short. However, we must face the natural consequences of heartbreak and broken trust that are an inevitable reality after an affair.

As the spouse who had an affair, you are asking for a vast amount of forgiveness. When you humble yourself and approach your spouse with a repentant, honest, and contrite heart, they will be more prone to forgive you quickly and trust you over time. Please remember that we all process things at different rates and experience various emotions, so give your spouse the time and space to cope so they can come to a place of forgiveness in their heart. Then, make it your mission to be honest and consistent in your words and actions to regain their trust every day.

Again, no spouse causes the other to have an affair, and an affair is never warranted, but we all fall short of being the perfect spouse. As it says in James 4:10, "Humble yourselves before the Lord, and he will lift you up in honor." Nothing is impossible with God... even saving a marriage after an affair. I highly encourage you both to see a Christian counselor on a regular basis and attend a crisis marriage retreat or conference.

Saving your marriage after an affair is not an easy road, and it will take everything you both have to fight for it, but your spouse and marriage are worth fighting for! It is our hope and prayer at XO Marriage that you and your spouse experience full restoration and healing in your marriage.

> **Nothing is impossible with God... even saving a marriage after an affair.**

How to Become a Trust-Builder

We all have a role to play in building trust. If you're married, you can do your part by living with complete honesty and integrity. Admit it when you've blown it. Through your consistent actions, show your spouse that you're the safest place on earth for them. Follow through on your promises.

For all of us, let's live with integrity in all of our relationships. Let's make it as easy as possible for our loved ones to arrive at the Comfort Stage with us because we've shown them we can be trusted. When we do mess up, let's actively work to rebuild trust.

Perhaps you're feeling called to do even more in this area. Maybe you are ready to step out in faith and provide help, hope, and mediation to couples who are currently struggling in these areas. Our ministry has launched a Mediators Institute where we offer training to individuals who want to become certified and equipped to guide others through the healing process. If you want to learn more about how you can equip yourself to make a life-changing difference for others, visit xomediator.com.

Questions to Consider:

1. Where do you believe you and your spouse are in The Five Stages of Trust? Be sure each of you shares your opinion on this and talk about it honestly.

2. If you aren't at the Comfort Stage quite yet, what would help both of you to get there? What behaviors do you personally need to change? What changes would you like your spouse to make?

3. Did someone close to you break your trust in the past? If so, who? How has this experience of betrayal affected the way you see and treat your spouse? Are you possibly holding what someone else did to you against your spouse? If so, pray that God would help you release this and heal from it. Apologize to your spouse and tell them about your past experience with betrayal.

4. Have you been unfaithful to your spouse? If so, have you ever told them? If not, pray about it first and

confess it to the Lord, repent, and seek His forgiveness. Then, tell your spouse about it at a time when you are both alone and can talk through it. Be prepared to answer any and all of their questions and seek your spouse's forgiveness. Ask your spouse what you need to do to regain their trust and do it. Also, consider setting up an appointment with one of our marriage coaches or mediators at XO Marriage by going to xomarriage. com/help. You can and will get through this!

CHAPTER 8

YOUR THOUGHT LIFE
AND YOUR SEX LIFE

An FBI Agent who worked in the field of stopping counter-feit currencies was once asked how much time he spent examining counterfeit money. His response surprised the questioner. He said, "I barely spend any time at all looking at counterfeit money. I spent most of my time studying every nuance of genuine currency. If I know all there is to know about the real thing, it's much easier to spot a counterfeit."

In this chapter, we want to talk about the power of allow-ing God's truth to renew your minds because your thought life is powerfully tied to your sex life. This mental renewal happens when we allow Scripture to guide our way and be the compass by which we chart our course. In the epilogue, we've put together a collection of some of our favorite Scriptures that have helped renew our own minds and marriage over the years.

In addition to the truth of Scripture, we also need to have a true understanding of how God designed our brains as men and women. Our most powerful sexual organs are not our genitals; they're our brains. Developing a deeper understanding of your own individual mental wiring will help you both safeguard your marriage from counterfeit love and untrue thoughts that can cause division and unnecessary conflict between you and your spouse.

When our minds are healthy, our thoughts can be the strongest tools we have to keep unity in our marriage—specifically in our sex lives. When our thought processes are broken up, our minds can trap us in a prison of unhealthy fantasies and untrue perspectives. If you want healthy sex, you need to have a healthy mind. It's that simple.

The Mind: The Most Powerful Human Sex Organ

Sin never stays in the compartment you build for it. The sexual fantasies you play on repeat in your brain can't stay in your mind forever without impacting other aspects of your life. The Bible tells us that as a person thinks in his heart, so is he (Proverbs 23:7 NKJV). In other words, our thought life will shape our real life. Our thoughts create the roadmap of our lives and our relationships. Everything we do—good or bad—begins in the mind long before it's acted out. The truth we put into our minds has great power, but the counterfeit messages we choose to believe also have power.

> If you want healthy sex, you need to have a healthy mind. It's that simple.

When the apostle Paul encouraged the Philippian church to "think about things that are excellent and worthy of praise" (Philippians 4:8), he was talking about much more than the power of positive thinking. He was reminding them—and us—that the frontlines of spiritual warfare exist between our ears. The brain is the most powerful sex organ of all.

As we were reading, researching, soul-searching, and praying about what needed to be included in this book, we quickly realized that we didn't just need to focus on what people are doing with their genitals, but we also needed to focus on what's happening in their minds. All sexual activity (and sexual sin) begins with thoughts. Breaking bad habits and starting healthy habits all begins in the mind. The more we can understand what we are thinking and feeling, the more we'll be able to help ourselves and others make wise and healthy choices.

While we both have some graduate school and seminary experience, and Ashley is currently working on her Masters in Biblical Counseling (MABC), we are not psychologists or neuroscientists, so we needed to consult with the professionals on this aspect of the book. Part of our research included an interview with our good friend Shaunti Feldhahn, a bestselling author and brilliant researcher on issues related to human relationships. She and her husband, Jeff, are both cited in this book, and their research and insights have helped us tremendously.

Shaunti shared with us some brilliant and thought-provoking insights about differences in the male and female thought processes and how these differences impact human behavior. She shared cutting-edge neurological research that showed differ-

> **The frontlines of spiritual warfare exist between our ears. The brain is the most powerful sex organ of all.**

ences in male versus female brain scans when people were shown images of an attractive person of the opposite sex.

Completely different parts of the brain would light up on the scan for each gender. We'll summarize Shaunti's insights in laymen's terms, but you can get the full scope of her ground-breaking research in the book she coauthored with Craig Gross, *Through a Man's Eyes: Helping Women Understand the Visual Nature of Men.*[17]

Shaunti explained that while men and women both find pleasure in looking at an attractive person of the opposite sex, and both genders can be tempted by visual lust or pornography, there are some major differences. A woman's brain lights up in the prefrontal cortex, which is sort of the Grand Central Station of the brain. From there, she remains in control of what she chooses to do with those images. She can choose to dwell on them or discard them, but the process is logical, and she typically feels empowered to do what she wishes with those mental images.

For women, Shaunti explained, the mental fantasies aren't usually tied directly to the visual act of sex alone (although they can be). Women can obviously be tempted by pornography, and a growing number of women are consumers of porn, but porn still largely remains an industry produced by men and for men. Women's fantasies are more nuanced than just the act itself. When it comes to processing fantasies, the female brain seems to have a more complex process than the cause and effect process males' fantasies tend to follow.

Women's fantasies are often about getting caught up in the

---

17 Shaunti Feldhahn and Craig Gross, *Through a Man's Eyes: Helping Women Understand the Visual Nature of Men* (Colorado Springs: Multnomah, 2015).

romance and adventure of it, with sex being only one aspect. For this reason, steamy romance novels with no pictures at all tend to find a much larger audience among female readers than they do with males. Even though female fantasies leave more to the imagination than the vulgar, visual bluntness of porn, these female romance fantasies can still be very damaging because it causes women to fantasize about intimate scenarios with other men instead of their own husband in the same way porn causes men to fantasize about intimate acts with other women, like we discussed earlier.

For men and boys, the process is completely different. When the image of an attractive woman or any sexualized image enters his brain, it doesn't start at the prefrontal cortex. It lights up the base of his brain, which triggers a more primal reaction, and it can feel like mental warfare for him to try to wrench those images or thoughts out of his mind before they start playing on a sexualized highlight reel in his brain.

This process may be different for men, but this *doesn't* mean men are powerless against their thought lives. It simply means men will usually have to be more vigilant against sexual imagery and more intentional about renewing their minds. As Martin Luther said, "You can't keep a bird from flying over your head, but you can keep it from building a nest in your hair."

Luther was talking about our thought lives. We can't always control which thoughts or images shoot through our brains, but even though it might cause temptation, we get to choose which thoughts and images we allow to dwell there.

Max Lucado shared a similar analogy in his bestselling

book *Anxious for Nothing.* He gave the analogy of your mind as an airport, and the airplanes represent all the different thoughts, images, and worries that are coming and going at all times. He challenged the reader to realize we hold the power as the air traffic controller of our minds. We ultimately determine which thoughts "land" and which ones fly away.[18]

God has indeed given us great power in our minds, and, in His wisdom, He also created unique differences in how men and women process things. While these differences are ultimately a good thing, they can create unintentional disrespect and miscommunication when males and females are unaware these differences exist.

Some misconceptions relate directly to the different ways males and females process images of the opposite sex. In his book *For Young Men Only,* Jeff Feldhahn conducted hundreds of interviews with teen boys and teen girls. He found that most boys assumed that when girls dressed in tight clothes, they were intentionally doing so to invite sexual advances or to induce sexual fantasies in the boys who saw them. The boys assumed that the girls knew that boys would look at any bare skin or tight clothes in sexualized terms, and, therefore, the girls "must" want to be viewed through a sexualized lens.

When Jeff interviewed girls about this same topic, most girls were horrified and shocked that boys would think this way. The majority of girls said they chose their clothes based primarily on what was in fashion, and it never occurred to them that boys

---

18 Max Lucado, *Anxious for Nothing: Finding Calm in a Chaotic World* (Nashville: Thomas Nelson, 2017), 121.

would view them or their clothing in a sexual way. Most girls were repulsed by the idea of boys thinking of them as objects of lust during masturbation. In fact, only 4% of girls reported choosing their clothes with a motive of attracting sexual attention, while 90% of boys thought the girls *were* dressing to get sexual attention. This is one of many examples of how misperceptions can cause unintentional tension and disrespect.[19]

Just to be clear, it's inappropriate for a boy to objectify a girl, regardless of what she's wearing, even if she's among the 4% dressing provocatively to intentionally gain sexual attention. I'm not going to dive into the minefield of debate on how girls should dress or what they should be doing differently to create healthy dynamics in coed relationships. Those are subjects for another book by another author. The one bit of commentary I will share is that most girls and women would think about their wardrobes in a different way if they fully knew what was happening in the male brain.

Males might be hardwired with a visual temptation to lust, but while the temptation might be inevitable, lust is always optional. In *Through a Man's Eyes,* Shaunti summarized this concept well by stating, "Although neuroscience shows that the first reaction is instinctive and biological rather than voluntary, the next step is always a choice."[20]

Having a basic understanding of how God wired us as men and women is one important aspect of the mutual

19 Jeff Feldhahn and Eric Rice, *For Young Men Only: A Guy's Guide to the Alien Gender* (Colorado Springs: Multnomah, 2008), 136.

20 Feldhahn and Gross, *Through a Man's Eyes*, 23.

respect and understanding necessary for great sex within healthy marriages. Through communication with your spouse, healthy habits, focusing on the positive (as we're told to do in Philippians 4:8), and continuous growth, you can bring health to your thought life and your sex life. Always remember that your thought life and your sex life are inextricably interconnected.

When Your Thoughts Pull You Away

I (Ashley) remember the conversation vividly. My friends and I were driving to the beach for a girls' trip. In a rare moment of silence, one friend blared out that she was going to leave her husband because she didn't love him anymore. As I listened to her explain how the spark was gone, sex wasn't good anymore, and they had both been bored with each other for a long time, I silently prayed that God would give the rest of us the words to help our hurting friend give her husband and her marriage another chance.

After some awkward silence, my other friend and I shared with her that every marriage has seasons of disappointment, frustration, and grind. Sometimes, we bring it on ourselves with bad choices or careless mistakes. Other times, we're blindsided by an unforeseen catastrophe. It's easy to point fingers during those times. It's easy to shut down, stop talking, and internalize bitterness or shame. Those moments—when our hearts are broken, and we have thousands of words left unspoken—are the very moments we need to lean into our spouse the most.

This world tells us that love is a feeling that can come and go. If this is true, then love will fail us every time, and it will never be enough to hold a marriage together. Thankfully, this is not at all how God defines love. In 1 Corinthians 13, Paul writes that true love is unconditional. It doesn't keep a record of wrongs. It protects us. It heals us.

True love never fails us. Even so, there may be moments we feel like giving up on our spouse and ending our marriage. Why is this? It all has to do with our mindset.

If we don't foresee hope and healing in our future, we don't want to put in the work and take the time to get to the root issues. We'd rather just start over, but what we fail to see and understand is that marriage is a lasting commitment that we will always carry with us, regardless of whether or not we move on. God designed it this way. It's not something we can just shake off and forget.

When we marry, we pledge to give every part of ourselves to our spouse, and we trust them to do the same. In our world today, this is frowned upon because it means we have to be completely vulnerable and put our hearts on the line. This is the beautiful mystery of marriage. When both partners do this to the best of their ability—

> **There may be moments we feel like giving up on our spouse and ending our marriage. Why is this? It all has to do with our mindset.**

baring souls before one another, holding nothing back—there is an incredible, intimate union that forms.

The more we pursue God and one another, the tighter the

bond becomes. I think most of us go into our marriages wanting this amazing union with our partner, but life gets in the way, and we forget to be intentional with our time. Eventually, our marriage gets put on the back burner, but this is counter to what God wants for our marriage and family.

When we are bored, disillusioned, and frustrated with our marriage, our minds can go to a dark, hopeless place. However, instead of allowing these thoughts to pull us away, we need to reach out for help. We must be willing to fight for our marriage. It certainly takes both the husband and wife to make it work, but we must be willing to take the first step.

My friend ultimately decided to recommit to her marriage and to trust her commitment more than her feelings. She and her husband even committed to a 30-Day Sex Challenge, where they made love every day for a month. It was awkward at first, but by the end of the first week, they were acting like a couple of honeymooners again. They'd be the first to tell you that it takes much more than sex to build a strong marriage, but it's very difficult to build a strong marriage without it. They both committed to reconnecting both inside and outside the bedroom, and today their marriage is stronger than it's ever been.

> **It takes much more than sex to build a strong marriage, but it's very difficult to build a strong marriage without it.**

Remember, as a husband and wife, you have vowed to be each other's partner, lover, best friend, encourager, accountability, and person to lean on when the other is weak. Marriage is a beautiful, lifelong partnership when we allow it to be, but we can't give up when it gets hard. We must press on. Let's not wonder how things could have been.

Dave and I certainly don't have a perfect marriage, nor do we have all the answers, but we know who does. I'm thankful that God doesn't abandon us when we have marital problems. He was right there for my friend when she needed Him most, and He is there for you and your spouse as well!

If you feel like giving up on your marriage right now, please take this to heart. There is hope. Don't let the lies make you quit. Don't believe the counterfeits. Find a marriage counselor and take the steps necessary to rebuild your marriage. It can get better when you both are committed to making it better and allow God to do the rest. You don't have to figure it out on your own.

Change Your Perspective

In 2012, a talented up-and-coming screenwriter named Jennifer Lee was completing work on a Disney movie called *Wreck-It Ralph* when she was invited to come play a big role on Disney's newest project. The new movie would be called *Frozen*, and it would be unlike anything the studio had ever produced. Tens of millions of dollars had already been invested into the project, but it hit a roadblock. They were close to pulling the plug altogether.

The movie was facing many setbacks, but one of the most urgent was the storyline. The plot seemed stuck. The characters weren't developing, and the songs weren't coming. Lee was brought in to help lead the writing effort and to codirect the film, which also made her Disney's first female feature film director ever.

Lee carefully studied the script and scrutinized the characters. She quickly realized that the story had unlimited potential, but before they could move forward, the writers needed to reimagine one key character. Up until that point, the main character of Elsa had been a villain. She was Hans Christian Andersen's cold and remorseless Snow Queen with no redeemable characteristics.

Lee brilliantly proposed that the story would only work if Elsa became one of the story's heroes. Like all heroes, she would be complicated and imperfect, but her heart would be good, and, in the end, she would be a vital part of creating a happy ending. Once the character of Elsa was reimagined and rewritten, the rest of the story came together perfectly. The songs began to flow. They were belting out "Let It Go" in no time.

The rest is cinematic history. Lee and her team at Disney created one of the most beloved and successful movies in history, spawning a multibillion-dollar franchise, including music, books, toys, costumes, spinoffs, a sequel, theme park rides, and a Broadway musical. You're probably humming a *Frozen* song in your head right now.

We share this story because we see some important parallels between the film's progress and our collective progress around the issues of unlearning the world's counterfeit messages about love and recommitting to God's truth. There is certainly so much to be done, and trying to solve this global problem all at once seems as overwhelming as charging into a raging forest fire armed only with a small squirt gun, but what if we took a different approach? What if, like Lee's approach to *Frozen*, we need to begin by simply reimaging one key character in the story?

The key character in this story is you (and us too). What if each of us reimagined the roles and responsibilities we have in bringing resolution to the sexual and relational baggage in our own lives, in our own marriages, and in the world around us? What if we allowed the Holy Spirit to do a new work in us and through us? Our lives, our marriages, and future generations could be better if we'll allow God to help us reimagine our own part in the story.

The Secrets of Happy Couples

One of the most damaging lies many couples believe is that true happiness in marriage is impossible, or perhaps it's only available for a lucky few. So many couples are settling for an unhappy marriage because they've convinced themselves there's no path forward to real and sustained happiness with their spouse. This is perhaps the most widely believed myth about marriage in our time.

We were reminded of this prevalent, negative mindset when we went on a trip earlier this year to celebrate a birthday. For big birthdays and big celebrations, we've always

> **What if each of us reimagined the roles and responsibilities we have in bringing resolution to the sexual and relational baggage in our own lives, in our own marriages, and in the world around us?**

valued time away together more than store-bought gifts. We love sharing new adventures. From the time we arrived at the hotel and throughout our stay, multiple staff members asked us, "Are you honeymooners?"

"No," we'd reply. "We've been married for 20 years."

"That's amazing!" They'd say, "You seem like honeymooners. We never see couples who are happy like you if they've been married very long."

Wow. What a sad thought! Do people really think that happiness in marriage is destined to fade with time? We've never bought into that myth. We've always believed a marriage should age like a fine wine, getting sweeter with time. Our marriage is far from perfect, but we can truly say we are very happy, and our happiness has grown deeper over the past two decades of marriage.

People will sometimes ask us what the "secret" is to a happy marriage. We've discovered through the years that happiness in marriage is possible for every couple, but it's not just about one secret. As far as we can tell from our own experience and learning from the experiences of others, there are ten distinct secrets of happy couples, and if you implement these principles in your own marriage, you will undoubtedly experience more happiness too.

> **One of the most damaging lies many couples believe is that true happiness in marriage is impossible, or perhaps it's only available for a lucky few.**

We want to share these secrets with you because they shouldn't be secrets at all. Everyone should have access to the truth that a happy marriage is within their reach. In no particular order, here are ten practical ways to cultivate a happier marriage:

1. Be quick to apologize and quick to offer grace to each other.

Someone once said that being in love means never having to say you're sorry. Whoever said that has probably been divorced five times! The truth is that we must be humble enough to quickly and wholeheartedly admit fault when we've blown it. We must also be quick to offer forgiveness and grace when our spouse apologizes. We can't keep score of each other's wrongs or use past mistakes as ammunition in arguments. We must forgive, work to rebuild the trust that was damaged, and move forward. Holding a grudge makes you bitter. Forgiveness sets you free.

2. Make laughter the soundtrack of your marriage.

Even in the difficult seasons of marriage, there is always a reason to laugh together. We believe a lack of laughter in a marriage is like a lack of fuel in a vehicle. You need to fill up your marriage with laughter to keep it running! If laughter has faded in your home, then look for ways to get it back on track. Put "fun" back on the calendar. Be playful and flirtatious with each other. Every marriage needs a lot of laughter, and laughing together is one of the most intimate and enjoyable acts a couple can share. Even if it starts with just watching reruns of your favorite sitcom together, start doing things that will bring more laughter.

3. Learn from other couples, but don't compare your marriage to anyone else's.

The "comparison trap" is a killer of happiness. If you find yourself scrolling through social media comparing your struggles to the airbrushed highlight reels of other people, then you're never going to feel happy or content with your own life. It's healthy to learn from other people (especially our mentors), but it's unhealthy to try to measure your life or marriage against theirs. God's plans for you are masterfully unique.

4. Prioritize your sex life.

It takes much more than sex to build a strong marriage, but it is nearly impossible to build a strong marriage without it. Prioritize your spouse's sexual needs. If your spouse is the one with the higher drive, then work to meet their need since you are the only legitimate source on earth where that need can be met. With prioritizing your sex life, don't prioritize just the act itself but also more affection, foreplay, flirtation, and celebration of each other. Work to find solutions when you face setbacks in your health or sex life and be patient and tender with each other when insecurities or limitations occur. Sex is a gift from God that's meant to be enjoyed in marriage, so enjoy it!

5. Cultivate a culture of gratitude in your marriage. Say "thank you" often.

Thank each other often and show genuine appreciation for all your spouse does. Be thankful to God as well for the gifts in your life. An attitude of gratitude is one of the biggest keys to happiness.

When you choose to be thankful for your life and for each other, every aspect of life can be enjoyed with more freedom.

6. Communicate about everything and never keep secrets from each other.

Communication is the lifeline keeping a marriage strong. You need to talk about everything. Make uninterrupted communication a regular part of your routine. Turn off your phones, remove distractions, and really talk. Don't keep secrets about anything. Secrecy is the enemy of intimacy. For us, one of our healthiest habits is going on a daily or nightly walk where we get some exercise and talk. Some of our best conversations happen on those walks.

7. Keep dreaming new dreams together and working toward shared goals.

In every season of marriage, you should always have something to look forward to. You should always have goals and dreams you're working together to reach. Keep dreaming together. You might be amazed at how creating some new dreams and goals can breathe fresh life into your relationship. Throughout our marriage, shared goals and dreams have been a constant connection point. These goals can be about anything from finances to fitness, to new ventures, to ministry, to parenting, and everything in between.

8. Develop a "Pro-Marriage" community.

Your marriage is going to start to resemble the marriages of the people you're hanging around the most, so make sure you choose friends who value marriage. For us, our community has always been rooted in the church. Our small group—where other couples in the same season of life come together, eat, hang out, pray, laugh, and encourage each other—meets regularly. We've also found older mentors who can teach us from their experience and younger couples whom we can mentor. Your community can be vital in helping you keep growing, but community takes work. Be intentional about developing these kinds of relationships.

9. Be patient with each other.

The Bible says, "Love is patient" (1 Corinthians 13:4), so we must always be patient with each other. Your spouse's timing is different from yours. Their needs are different. Their preferences are different. Be thankful for each other's differences and always be patient, loving, kind, and tenderhearted with each other, especially in these areas of differences. Instead of allowing your differences to be a source of conflict, make them a source of strength by celebrating each other's unique perspectives.

10. Make sure your faith in God is your unwavering foundation.

If this list was written in order, this would be number one! Through all the storms of life, our faith in Christ and His guidance has helped us stay strong. When you and your spouse commit to building your lives on a foundation of faith, you're making the wisest decision possible. In all the ups and downs of life, God will be your steady anchor. We believe there's no true happiness or health apart from Him, but in Him and through Him, *all* things are possible.

If you work together with your spouse to start doing (or keep doing) these ten things, we believe more health and happiness are in your future! Work together to identify the lies you've believed that have been holding you back from health and happiness. Once the lies are out of the way, the truth can set you free.

Questions to Consider:

1. What are your most consistent thoughts about your spouse, your marriage, and sex in general?

2. Which thoughts are helpful?

3. Which thoughts are harmful?

4. Do you have any thoughts that are pulling you away from your spouse and your marriage?

5. Do you have any thoughts that are hindering your sex life? Negative thoughts or insecurities about your body, your spouse's body, performance, comparison, etc.? Think and pray about these things and talk about them with your spouse. Ask God to replace these negative and harmful thoughts with more positive and productive ones.

CHAPTER 9

THE SEX TALK THAT COULD CHANGE YOUR LIFE

It's time to put what we've learned into action. In this short, final chapter, we want to guide you through an exercise that truly has the potential to change your life. If you haven't answered the Questions to Consider at the end of each chapter yet, we encourage you to start your conversation there—and in order. First, answer these questions for yourself, and then answer them with your spouse. It could spark the most vulnerable and intimate conversation about sex you've ever had. If you have been following along and have already discussed the questions at the end of each of the previous chapters, then you are ready to set some sexual goals together. Below are some questions to consider when setting some sexual goals for your marriage:

1. How would our sex life look different if we were doing everything I wanted to do in terms of frequency, variety, etc.?

2. What is one thing I could change about my actions or attitudes that would make me a better lover to my spouse?

3. (Without blaming your spouse) What factors are currently holding me back from experiencing more sexual intimacy and connection in our marriage?

4. How are my current sexual goals and desires shaping my views and experiences with sex?

Once you've had the chance to reflect on these questions for yourself, as a next step, we challenge you to go back through this same list with your spouse. It might seem terrifying to have such a vulnerable and "naked" conversation with your spouse, but we believe this could be one of the most important conversations you've ever had. It most likely won't be just one conversation. It will start with one conversation that will lead to a series of conversations that reshape how you talk about sex.

Married couples need to normalize talking about their sex lives. In the work we do with married couples, we've found that people are thinking about sex a lot, but they're barely talking about it at all. In some ways, the act of talking about sex can feel more intimate and vulnerable than the act of having sex. If you have these conversations, we believe the communication will enhance your bond with your spouse both inside and outside the bedroom.

Married couples need to normalize talking about their sex lives.

Hopefully, you discussed many of these things before marriage, but even still, there are probably certain subjects these lists of questions address that will reveal some previously undisclosed information. Since these conversations might lead you into some uncharted waters, it's important to set a few ground rules before diving in to make sure the conversation is a safe space instead of a potential minefield. Here are a few things to keep in mind:

- Schedule this conversation in a safe, private space where you won't be interrupted. It could be on your back porch or at your kitchen table as long as the kids aren't home and the phones are turned off. Whether you have this conversation at home or somewhere away from home, you need to be able to engage with each other in these important questions without distractions or interruptions.

- Make sure you share as many details of your sexual past with your spouse as they want to hear, but also be sensitive, knowing these details could create unwanted visualizations and insecurities. Ask in advance how detailed they would like you to be with the specifics of the stories.

- Give each other a lot of grace, compassion, and reassurance. Never shame each other over past choices (or present struggles and insecurities) but be a safe place for each other. Remember that in Christ, the Bible says we are "a new creation" (2 Corinthians 5:17 NIV), and we're no longer defined by the sins of our past.

- Talk about things you'd like to do differently to enhance the intimacy and mutual pleasure in the bedroom. Again, don't shame each other or blame each other for the ways your spouse's desires and drives are different from your own.

- Be very uplifting and complimentary of each other. Let your spouse know how much you desire them, adore them, and respect them.

- At both the start of your conversation and again at the end, hold hands and pray out loud for each other. Thank God for your spouse. Thank God for your marriage. Thank God for His grace. Ask Him to bless, protect, and guide you in all parts of your marriage. The act of praying together is one of the most intimate moments a couple can share. It will help create the right tone for this important conversation.

We challenge you to call your spouse right now and set up a time to have this conversation. Like we've said, we truly believe it could be life-changing for you and one of the most intimate and important moments you've ever shared as a couple. Once you both realize that your marriage is the safest place on earth to address your secrets and insecurities, nothing can hold you back. And once you realize Jesus is offering to carry the baggage for you and your spouse and is there to support you every step of the way, you can experience life, sex, and marriage with a freedom you'd never thought was possible. Don't settle for anything less!

We truly hope this book has helped you replace counterfeit forms of love with the truth of God's perfect plan for your marriage. We pray you've gained some practical tools you can use to build a stronger marriage and a better sex life. We hope the world's counterfeits have lost their influence in your heart and your home, and God's truth has ushered in a new season of growth, healing, and renewal.

You've reached the end of this book, but the journey toward healthy relationships is a lifelong quest. We're honored to be on this journey with you. Thank you again for joining us. We hope to stay connected to you through our *Naked Marriage* podcast, social media, live events, and other resources at xomarriage.com. We pray God's continued blessings for you. The best is yet to come!

Once you realize Jesus is offering to carry the baggage for you and your spouse and is there to support you every step of the way, you can experience life, sex, and marriage with a freedom you'd never thought was possible.

EPILOGUE

SCRIPTURES TO GUIDE YOUR WAY

As we end this book, we want to leave with you with some truths from God's Word that have shaped our own marriage over the years. We were once given sage advice from an old preacher. He said with a grin, "When you write, make sure you use a lots of Scripture. That way, you'll know at least something you said is actually true!"

That's good advice. That's why we've included Scripture throughout this book. We want to make sure the timeless truth of God's Word is the unchanging standard by which we build a foundation for life and relationships. In a world of ever-shifting standards, we need an unchanging compass now, more than ever. We know that we are imperfect, and, like all people, we can be prone to falling for counterfeits, but God's Word never leads us astray. We're told in the Bible, "Every word of God is flawless; he is a shield to those who take refuge in him" (Proverbs 30:5).

As you read and reflect on these timeless truths from God's Word, we hope these words will bring you as much comfort and direction as they've brought to us through the years:

Now the man and his wife were both naked, but they felt no shame. (Genesis 2:25)

Then God blessed them and said, "Be fruitful and multiply. Fill the earth and govern it. Reign over the fish in the sea, the birds in the sky, and all the animals that scurry along the ground." (Genesis 1:28)

So now I am giving you a new commandment: Love each other. Just as I have loved you, you should love each other. (John 13:34)

A person standing alone can be attacked and defeated, but two can stand back-to-back and conquer. (Ecclesiastes 4:12)

The man who finds a wife finds a treasure, and he receives favor from the Lord. (Proverbs 18:22)

Get rid of all bitterness, rage, anger, harsh words, and slander, as well as all types of evil behavior. Instead, be kind to each other, tenderhearted, forgiving one another, just as God through Christ has forgiven you. (Ephesians 4:31–32)

Understand this, my dear brothers and sisters: You must all be quick to listen, slow to speak, and slow to get angry. (James 1:19)

Charm is deceptive, and beauty does not last; but a woman who fears the Lord will be greatly praised. Reward her for all she has done. Let her deeds publicly declare her praise. (Proverbs 31:30–31)

Love is patient and kind. Love is not jealous or boastful or proud or rude. It does not demand its own way. It is not irritable, and it keeps no record of being wronged. (1 Corinthians 13:4–5)

Don't copy the behavior and customs of this world, but let God transform you into a new person by changing the way you think. Then you will learn to know God's will for you, which is good and pleasing and perfect. (Romans 12:2)

You have heard the commandment that says, "You must not commit adultery." But I say, anyone who even looks at a woman with lust has already committed adultery with her in his heart. (Matthew 5:27–28)

Love prospers when a fault is forgiven, but dwelling on it separates close friends. (Proverbs 17:9)

The husband should fulfill his wife's sexual needs, and the wife should fulfill her husband's needs. The wife gives authority over her body to her husband, and the husband gives authority over his body to his wife. Do not deprive each other of sexual relations. (1 Corinthians 7:3–5a)

Don't worry about anything; instead, pray about everything. Tell God what you need, and thank him for all he has done. Then you will experience God's peace, which exceeds anything we can understand. His peace will guard your hearts and minds as you live in Christ Jesus. (Philippians 4:6–7)

As the Scriptures say, "A man leaves his father and mother and is joined to his wife, and the two are united into one." This is a great mystery, but it is an illustration of the way Christ and the church are one. So again, I say, each man must love his wife as he loves himself, and the wife must respect her husband. (Ephesians 5:31–33)

For you have been called to live in freedom, my brothers and sisters. But don't use your freedom to satisfy your sinful nature. Instead, use your freedom to serve one another in love. (Galatians 5:13)

Love each other with genuine affection, and take delight in honoring each other. (Romans 12:10)

Three things will last forever—faith, hope, and love—and the greatest of these is love. (1 Corinthians 13:13)

And we know that God causes everything to work together for the good of those who love God and are called according to his purpose for them. (Romans 8:28)

God saved you by his grace when you believed. And you can't take credit for this; it is a gift from God. Salvation is not a reward for the good things we have done, so none of us can boast about it. For we are God's masterpiece. He has created us anew in Christ Jesus, so we can do the good things he planned for us long ago. (Ephesians 2:8–10)

But the Holy Spirit produces this kind of fruit in our lives: love, joy, peace, patience, kindness, goodness, faithfulness, gentleness, and self-control. There is no law against these things! (Galatians 5:22–23)

The thief's purpose is to steal and kill and destroy. My purpose is to give them a rich and satisfying life. (John 10:10)

So don't worry about these things, saying, "What will we eat? What will we drink? What will we wear?" These things dominate the thoughts of unbelievers, but your heavenly Father already knows all your needs. Seek the Kingdom of God above all else, and live righteously, and he will give you everything you need. (Matthew 6:31–33)

But if we confess our sins to him, he is faithful and just to forgive us our sins and to cleanse us from all wickedness. (1 John 1:9)

Jesus told him, "I am the way, the truth, and the life. No one can come to the Father except through me." (John 14:6)

But God showed his great love for us by sending Christ to die for us while we were still sinners. And since we have been made right in God's sight by the blood of Christ, he will certainly save us from God's condemnation. (Romans 5:8–9)

And now, dear brothers and sisters, one final thing. Fix your thoughts on what is true, and honorable, and right, and pure, and lovely, and admirable. Think about things that are excellent and worthy of praise. (Philippians 4:8)

He gives power to the weak and strength to the powerless. Even youths will become weak and tired, and young men will fall in exhaustion. But those who trust in the Lord will find new strength. They will soar high on wings like eagles. They will run and not grow weary. They will walk and not faint. (Isaiah 40:29–31)

But you are not like that, for you are a chosen people. You are royal priests, a holy nation, God's very own possession. As a result, you can show others the goodness of God, for he called you out of the darkness into his wonderful light. (1 Peter 2:9)

All Scripture is inspired by God and is useful to teach us what is true and to make us realize what is wrong in our lives. It corrects us when we are wrong and teaches us to do what is right. God uses it to prepare and equip his people to do every good work. (2 Timothy 3:16–17)

Give all your worries and cares to God, for he cares about you. (1 Peter 5:7)

Then Jesus said, "Come to me, all of you who are weary and carry heavy burdens, and I will give you rest. Take my yoke upon you. Let me teach you, because I am humble and gentle at heart, and you will find rest for your souls." (Matthew 11:28–29)

The Lord is my shepherd; I have all that I need. (Psalm 23:1)

This means that anyone who belongs to Christ has become a new person. The old life is gone; a new life has begun! (2 Corinthians 5:17)

For I can do everything through Christ, who gives me strength. (Philippians 4:13)

"For I know the plans I have for you," says the Lord. "They are plans for good and not for disaster, to give you a future and a hope." (Jeremiah 29:11)

Jesus came and told his disciples, "I have been given all authority in heaven and on earth. Therefore, go and make disciples of all the nations, baptizing them in the name of the Father and the Son and the Holy Spirit. Teach these new disciples to obey all the commands I have given you. And be sure of this: I am with you always, even to the end of the age." (Matthew 28:18–20)

As you continue the journey of growing closer to God and closer to your spouse, let Scripture lead the way. The more of God's Word you hide in your heart, the more of a foundation you'll have to weather the storms of life. Remember that in all seasons of life and marriage, Jesus is with you, and He will never leave you nor forsake you.

ACKNOWLEDGEMENTS

There are so many people who have impacted our own story and also have helped give life to this book. Before we list out some important friends, colleagues, and mentors who have shaped *The Counterfeit Climax*, we want to thank YOU for taking the time to read this book. By reading, applying and sharing the message of this book, you've partnered with us in this work of building healthier lives and healthier marriages. Thank you!

Our deepest gratitude and appreciation go to XO Marriage's founding leaders, Jimmy and Karen Evans and Brent and Stephanie Evans. Their leadership and ongoing support make all our work at XO possible. We are truly honored to call the entire Evans family our friends and we're equally honored they've adopted us into the XO Marriage family. Brent gets an additional shoutout for coming up with the title "Counterfeit Climax," which we immediately loved.

We are deeply humbled and grateful to work alongside an incredible team of staff and marriage coaches at XO Marriage. This book may have our names on the front, but, like every aspect of this ministry, it was truly a team effort. We have the privilege of being a part of a world-class team of people who serve and lead wholeheartedly with authentic faith, tenacious grit, and contagious enthusiasm. We're sorry that all their names couldn't fit on the front cover, but the entire team at XO Marriage and XO Publishing was instrumental in this project.

We want to thank Karina Lopez and Dan Van who were this book's primary editors. Dan and Karina were a creative force helping to shape and improve the content of this book. We would also like to thank Joni Smith and Eric Gomez for their creative insights and encouragement throughout the writing process. Additionally, we thank *The Naked Marriage* podcast team of Marcus Bowen, Jonathan Armbruster, Noah Armbruster, Andrew Grekoff, Josey Edwards, McKaylee Maddox, and Eric Randall for their ongoing work and creativity in sharing this book's message through the podcast and other XO channels.

We are eternally grateful for the love and support of our family. We want to thank our parents, Brad and Karen Willis and Bill and Mary McCray for your lifelong love and support. We know they probably cringe or blush every time they have to hear their kids talking about sex, but they're really good sports about it! We also want to thank our siblings and our extended family for all you do for us. Special thanks to our precious sons Cooper, Connor, Chandler, and Chatham. We love you boys and all we do, we do for you. The greatest honor in our lives is the privilege of being your parents.

Our heartfelt gratitude also extends to our friends near and far who have helped shape the content of this book through your stories, your encouragement and your prayers. For those social media friends and *The Naked Marriage* podcast listeners whom we've never met in person but who have encouraged us, prayed for us, and shared our content with others, please know that your impact on this ministry and on our lives is profound. Thank you for your partnership in this work of building healthier marriages and pointing more people to God's love, grace, and peace.

Finally, and most importantly, we want to thank Jesus Christ, our Lord and Savior. He is the giver of all good things. In a world full of counterfeits, He is the embodiment of authenticity and truth.

Marriage Help

We understand that when your marriage is struggling, you need help in a timely manner. XO Marriage is here to support you and stand alongside you in the fight for your marriage. We offer two distinct services:

Coaching on Call
Offered at multiple lengths, these sessions are designed for couples or individuals who are in crisis and need immediate help. Specializing in marital crisis intervention, our team is available to meet you in your time of need to listen with compassion and understanding, provide wise objective counsel, and help you navigate the best plan of action to start the healing process.

Marriage Mediation
Our full day private one-on-one marriage mediation is designed for couples who are struggling with multiple issues and/or feeling hopeless about the future of their marriage. This intensive approach allows couples the extended time needed to fully process their primary issues without the interruption of time or hassle of scheduling multiple weekly sessions.

To learn more, visit **xomarriage.com/help**.

 **NOW**

Get exclusive access to the best marriage-building content on any device!

Watch classes, workshops, conferences, and live teachings from leading marriage experts in the comfort of your home.

Start your free trial today, for only $9/month!

xonow.com

Grow Closer Together

The XO Marriage Conference is designed to help you connect with your spouse and build a strong foundation for your relationship.

You'll hear from Christian marriage experts like Jimmy Evans, Dave and Ashley Willis, and many other leading speakers about the secrets to a healthy, thriving marriage. At XO, you can expect dynamic teachings, worship, and an inspiring environment that will help you and your spouse grow closer together and build a strong marriage.

xomarriage.com/conferences

When you give to XO Marriage, you're making an investment in your own marriage while helping us spread the message of hope that every person has a 100% chance of success in marriage.

Give today at xomarriage.com/give.